THE GREEN LANES

The Green Lanes

A Westmorland Childhood

Betty Emmaline Walker

Illustrated by Leslie Walker

William Sessions Limited
York, England

ISBN 1 85072 214 5

Printed in 10 on 12 point Palatino typeface
from Author's disk
by Sessions of York, The Ebor Press,
York YO31 9HS
England

CONTENTS

for Robin

Prologue

From the graceful arch of the old stone bridge over the river the lane leads up towards the wood, crossing the running little stream where we gathered watercress, and past the copse, once bright with flowers but now choked with waist-high grasses. The stream still rushes underground and leaps out onto slabby rocks in a cascade of sparkling bubbles to form the waterfall, before tumbling into the river.

We could never walk past it. We stood on the bottom bar of the wooden fence and leaned over, fascinated by the endless gushing of water, slightly heady and dizzy from watching the light dancing on the bouncing bubbles, and indeed would have leaned there indefinitely had not a gentle adult hand persuaded us to continue along the stony path which led to the massive oak tree, around whose vast rough trunk I would stretch my thin arms to see how far they would reach. Its branches make a great umbrella across the path, and the hedges on either side, once trimmed and laid neatly flat, are now tall, dense and uneven.

To the right is the farm. The gateway is unchanged, the curving stone outer walls are moss-covered, and across the earthworn courtyard the creeper on the front of the old house is thicker, but the pungent smell of cows and cowsheds is just the same, and even a cock bird still crows in mid-afternoon.

The lane slowly climbs and the ground to the left begins to fall sharply away down to the water. The river is shallow, clear and swiftly flowing, forming here and there trouty pools filled with bright green waving water ferns. There is always the sound of water here, lapping over stones, gurgling round rocks and old tree roots, and curving around grassy banks. In spate it is roaring and brown and splashing up creamy foam before entering the quieter waters which flow under the bridge.

THE GREEN LANES

In the grass verges and hedges are the earliest Spring flowers; dog's mercury, violets and stitchwort, to be followed in High Summer by honeysuckle and red campions, wild roses and meadowsweet. The path is now steeper and becomes what we knew as the Cart Road, and the Wood can be reached up a rough, tussocky bank. Here was the 'Salmon Hole' where the bank had been cut away in a half-moon shape, leaving it partly bare and uncovering rust-coloured earth. Hidden in the moss and grass was a robin's nest, feather-lined, with five pale brown eggs.

Up the bank, through ferns and bracken and a maze of hazel and sycamore trees, dead twigs snapping underfoot, the wood path leads to an ancient hedge. It is unexpectedly damp, the ground is black, thick with years of fallen leaves. Elderberry bushes abound, their sharp green leaves curtain out the sunlight. But in this quiet shady moistness is a sudden profusion of gold, – kingcups, globe flowers, and red and yellow mimulus.

Ahead lies the little cinder path through the wood, curving and still climbing. The drop down to the river is rockier and steeper than before. A slender wire fence strung between concrete posts provides safety from a fall. Trees on either side form a tunnel and dapple the sunlight. From the luscious undergrowth peep delicate, purple-veined pearly wood-sorrel, 'cuckoo's bread and cheese', and starry white wood anemones. And here is a favourite tree, easy to climb in those days, where one could sit among the branches, sometimes with a book, and dream away the afternoon, drowsy with the smell of the woodland floor, of warm grass, and the distant ripple of the river.

The path levels out onto a grassy clearing bounded by several oak trees. The brown hens and their brown-skinned owner have long since departed from the scene, and no one calls now at the back door with a basket over his arm full of big brown eggs at twelve for a shilling. There is still a little track leading through the bushes and down the slope to the back of Woodside Terrace and School House, but only someone who has lived here would know of it. The main path emerges from the clearing onto the rough, stony, unmade road, and suddenly we are in the village.

Over the years man has wrought changes here as inevitably he must, widening pathways, making new road surfaces, building new houses, and enlarging some of those already there. The new gardens are brilliant with exotic blooms beside the old cottage garden flowers and shrubs. But nature has wrought changes too. Some trees and paths have gone, others have grown and spread almost beyond recognition. The 'Salmon Hole' has disappeared as though it had never been there, and cars grind up the hill where once there was only an occasional farm cart. However there are those things which abide and which have not changed; the river, the bridge over it, the waterfall beside it, and the great drifts of bluebells through the woods.

It is late in May, – when the trees have at last all burst into leaf at the end of a long, cold Spring, when the broom is thick with yellow and when, in the early evening a while before sunset, an invisible hand has swept the sky clear of the remaining clouds, – that sounds and scents conjure up places and associations which are now lost, except in the mind's eye and in the imagination. Some are well remembered, some half forgotten and only on the fringe of memory; the certain notes of a blackbird late in the day; the strange pungent smell of the flowering currant; the breathless excitement of hide-and-seek as dusk is falling; clusters of pink and creamy hawthorn blossom; ice-skating in the moonlight; celandines and cowslips; gathering sticks and blackberries; all carry the special recall of a much loved garden and of woods and fields beyond.

I want to remember it as I experienced it in childhood, from the safety and protection of a loving and comfortable home; to remember that while I was so much part of it, yet I was set apart from it, due almost entirely to my mother's sound financial position and to her education, to her practical skills and her good taste. This, together with my father's gentlemanly quietness and bearing and his love for the countryside, made my childhood years in this small, out-of-the-way place seem idyllic. My surroundings were observed closely with eyes which had not yet recognised ugliness; eyes which found interest and beauty and fascination in everything around.

CHAPTER ONE

The Village

It was a hilly area. The steep sloping fields were full of sheep and cattle, and were scattered about with outcrops of limestone rock and old trees. On the southern fringe of the village were the woods. Quiet, shady and unfrequented they sheltered not only a population of small animals, moles, mice, voles and occasionally rabbits – some unfortunately falling prey from time to time to the village cats – but were home to large numbers of wild birds throughout the seasons.

The green lanes leading out of the village were bounded by dry stone walls covered with mosses and lichens and in varying stages of decrepitude, and by thorny hedges always cut and laid flat by men in thick hedging gloves.

The village of Mealbank was built on a long, steep winding hill with the river at the bottom of the hill and the Oxenholme to Carlisle railway at the top. It was always referred to as a village but it was, in fact, a hamlet, a backwater which somehow never had a signpost leading to it, and perhaps for that reason it attracted no visitors. The road was rough and stony, in dry weather full of dust, and in wet weather full of muddy puddles. An attempt had once been made to put a tar MacAdam surface onto it, but the little steamroller fell over on its side half way up the hill, and the problems which ensued in lifting it back onto its rollers were of such magnitude for the resources available that no further efforts were expended in this direction and the road remained in its un-made-up state.

There was no Church, no shop – no official one that is – no Public House, no Post Office or public telephone, no proper bus service and no railway station. So what was there in this apparent backwater? There was a post box, let into the wall of one of the cottages, so letters and cards could be posted provided you had stamps. Deliveries and collections were made twice a day; in the morning by Mr Towell on his bicycle, and in the afternoon by a nameless postman in a van.

There was the School, which will feature from time to time, and there was the Mill. The Mill had been, and still was in those days, the life blood of the village.

The lively waters of the River Mint had provided power for mills in the village for some six hundred years. At least four different mills have been recorded, but it is the Woollen Mill which plays an important part in my story.

It was the last link with Kendal's historic industry, begun in the fourteenth century when John Kemp, a woollen manufacturer from Flanders, settled in the town. Of course ever since sheep had been introduced onto the Lakeland Fells – too long ago for anyone to know just when – their wool had been used: it had been spun from the fleece and then woven by people in their own homes. But now a thriving industry was set up in the town, and the famous Kendal Green cloth was produced; though it must be said that it was rough, tough and coarse, and at first not fine enough to export.

By the sixteenth century the industry had given Kendal its coat of arms of wool hooks and teazles – hooks to stick into the bales of wool to drag them about to where they were needed, and teazles to comb and card the wool and to raise the nap on the cloth. Giving employment to most of the townspeople, it is not surprising that the motto under the coat of arms is 'Pannus mihi Panis', Wool is my Bread. And for almost two hundred years the village woollen mill had provided most of its inhabitants with the means of earning their living.

The houses and cottages in the village had been built for the employees by the mill owners in about 1850. Constructed in local grey limestone they were rather austere, with little if any adornment. Four small terraces of cottages were unevenly spaced up the winding hill from the Mill and the river. There were three larger houses, one known as Mill House was attached to the office block, another in the middle of the village was the Mill manager's house, and the third was the School House.

What the village lacked in general amenities was perhaps made up for to a certain extent by every house having a water closet, an extraordinary and rare luxury for a country community three miles from the town. Having said that, only the three larger houses had this facility within the house, others had to walk down the back garden to a separate stone building, and in fact the W.C's for ten of the houses at the lower end of the village were all housed in one communal toilet block, not unlike a modern public convenience but with each household having a key to its own private lavatory. Were you considered lucky to live next door to the toilet block, or was it more amenable to live at a distance, but have to walk, say, fifty yards or so when Nature called? Which indeed was preferable on a cold, dark, wet night?

The School, halfway between the river and the railway, served not only the educational needs of the little community but was the Methodist chapel as well. Next door was the School House, and it was here that my parents set up home after their marriage in 1919.

My father, Edmund Robinson, went to work at the Mill when he was eleven years old. His father, John Robinson, had died at the early age of thirty-eight, leaving my grandmother with seven children. It is probable that at the time of his death, two and possibly three of their daughters were already working at the Mill, about a mile-and-a-half from their home at The Laurels, Scalthwaiterigg Stocks. The family would not be destitute therefore, and to supplement the income a little further my grandmother took in washing.

It is not known, and therefore it can only be surmised, how the washing of clothes was done in that household. Certainly there would be no hot running water. All water would be heated on the fire in kettles and pans, unless there was a sett-pot, and I think that would be unlikely in a small cottage. There may not even have been a sink. So however the washing was done it would be a back-breaking task and extremely hard on the hands, as coarse washing soap of those days contained a lot of soda, and there was no soap powder or soap flakes. Flat irons heated at the fire were used to press and iron the clothes. My grandmother was paid half-a-crown for a basketful of washed and ironed clothes. Once a week she walked to Skelsmergh Church to scrub the chancel floor with paraffin. For this task she was paid one shilling. The journey there and back must have been at least three miles.

One of her bachelor brothers, Tom Metcalfe, came to live with the family. He occupied a small room at the back of the house. He was musical and played the fiddle and the melodeon. One of my cousins remembers peeping into his room and seeing the melodeon. Unfortunately one day the rockers of the rocking chair came into contact with the bellows of the instrument, "so that", said she, "finished that". He was said to be very fond of Granny's home-made rhubarb pie, but on one occasion was tactless enough to remark, "Eh, Lizzie, this pie isn't as good as you usually make", whereupon my exasperated grandmother threw what remained of it onto the fire.

He is said to have dug out and constructed Cross Lane from The Laurels to the village – to make the journey to the Mill shorter. This may well have been so, but it has also been said that Cross Lane was opened up to allow a new engine or boiler to be taken to the Mill, presumably before the road bridge over the river near to the Mill, and known as the New Bridge, was built.

Cross Lane was not a right of way, though I was never aware of that. To me it was one of the many green lanes which I knew so well and which I never tired of exploring. It was bounded on one side for part of its length by a high, rather precarious-looking dry-stone wall. By sticking my shoe toes into the gaps between the stones I could raise myself up high enough to put my arms on the top of the wall and look across to Scarfoot Cottages, to the bridge, the river, and in the distance to the steeple of Skelsmergh Church. Here, if my feet were firmly fixed between the stones, I could lean comfortably and absorb the familiar and satisfying scene, leap-frogging in imagination over the field, down to the river and across it, away to my right and to the north, up the Scar and Betty Scott Lane, and perhaps even to the top of Whinfell Beacon, which I knew was fifteen hundred feet high, and where – when a war ended victoriously or a new King or Queen was crowned – sticks and wood were dragged to the top and a great bonfire lit in celebration. It was some years later I learned that the original purpose of the beacon was to warn of coming raids by the marauding Scots.

Then if I gazed to the left and the south there was Kendal, always rather hazy and grey in the distance, and away beyond that I knew there was the sea. Not that it was visible from here, but I knew it was there because I had seen it from Paddy Lane, above the railway behind me. The centre of this panorama was rather more sobering. If I could fly like a jackdaw over the cottages at Scarfoot, and over the house known as Dodding Green where the Roman Catholic priest lived, I would alight on the steeple of Skelsmergh Church on top of the hill, and look down upon the busy main road from Kendal to Shap.

Nearer to the village the wall ended and both sides of Cross Lane became wooded. It was always rather dark and damp here. The close, thick growth of trees and shrubs and tangles of creepers precluded the light for much of the day, and if dusk was gathering as we made our way home – having perhaps strayed too far for too long – we ran quickly, darting glances from one side to the other, rather fearful of any fanciful monster which might be lurking in the darkness. In recent years the owner of the land has allowed the lane to return to woods, fields and meadows, and Cross Lane is no more. But for whatever purpose it was constructed it not only lessened the journey from the Stocks to the Mill by a good half-mile but also spared the walker the effort of climbing the steep hill up to Hayfell bridge, and negotiating the correspondingly steep incline down into the village.

Of Granny Robinson's five daughters who survived to adulthood, four married. The eldest, Anne, lived in Lancaster, and the second daughter Elizabeth lived in Bradford. They had married early and produced sons and daughters all much older than ourselves, and my own father had married what was then considered late. We saw our cousins from time to time when they visited the Aunts in the village and in Kendal, but they were marrying and having their own families while we were still schoolgirls, so their lives and ours at that time had little in common. The youngest daughter, Fanny, married and lived in Kendal and featured prominently in all our lives.

In the early nineteen-twenties my grandmother came with two of her daughters, Sarah Agnes, the only unmarried one, and Mary, a First World War widow, to live in a cottage in the village, a few yards from our own home.

CHAPTER TWO

School House

I think that the very first recollection I have is of sitting in my pram. It was a low, black, coach-built Marmet pram, one end of which let down so that it could also be used as a push chair. My mother would wheel the pram along the front garden path to the double gates and leave it a moment at the gate, which was always kept closed, while she opened the other to allow the pram to be pushed through onto the road. The gates and all the outside window sills of the house were painted Venetian red. The front door was painted white, and this was a very pleasing colour scheme against the grey limestone.

Two mature cypress trees grew on either side of the front gates, and around the perimeter of the garden were variegated laurel, holly, kerria (which we called Japanese Roses) and bushes which grew snowberries, which we were constantly warned not to eat. There were elaborate iron railings around part of the front garden which when the house was built extended in front of the school as far as the school door, but sometime during the nineteen-twenties the area in front of the school was cleared and the size of the garden was thus reduced.

During the Second World War, in 1940, an appeal was made for iron railings and gates to be given for melting down to make munitions – it was not compulsory and some people were unwilling to part with their railings, but my parents allowed theirs to be cut off at ground level and taken away. I think that my mother always regretted it. The hedge which was planted to replace the railings could never match their elegance.

Over the years laburnum trees, pink hawthorn bushes and a rustic archway were added to the garden. There was a lawn at the front and a rose-bed in the middle of it. Here it was that we put up the rectangular green-and-white striped tent on hot sunny days, and tea in the tent was one of our treats.

The garden at the back of the house was given over to the cultivation of fruit and vegetables and to the greenhouse. For a few years in the Twenties my father kept white fan-tailed pigeons here, and we had a round and quite pictur-esque pigeon cote. Steps went down from the back garden to the cellar which had been the original kitchen, with a vast fireplace and oven which was still in use when my parents took up residence. But they soon discovered to their horror that the other residents of this basement kitchen were cock-roaches. It was thought that the removal of the fireplace would also remove the cockroaches, so a man whose name was Bill was sent from the mill to take out the kitchen range. When my father returned from work on the day this opera-tion was carried out, and asked, "Well, Bill, did you find any cockroaches?", Bill is said to have replied, "Aye, Teddy, many a bloody million!" It was certainly the end of the cock-roaches, but my parents abandoned the cellar as a kitchen and moved upstairs to the ground floor.

The cellar became the wash-house and my father's work-shop. On the walls hung his tools and on the shelves were tins of nails and screws, paint and oil and all manner of things for the handyman. Here too he hung herbs and vari-ous wild plants to dry, later to be rubbed up and mixed with tobacco to be smoked in his pipe.

The cellar was also the scene of winemaking and the brewing of home-made beer, not always completely suc-cessful. There were times when we would be sitting in the room over the cellar, which was our dining room, and we would hear a loud bang. My father would go down to investigate and return with the news that the cork had burst from yet another bottle of beer and the contents had van-ished. Then there was the famous occasion when a barrel of home-brewed beer had been placed inside the kitchen door. One of my sister's boyfriends had just arrived when the bung blew out of the barrel, and the beer cascaded down the back door steps as the young man was coming up them.

The house looked larger than it really was. In addition to the newly-constructed kitchen off the dining room there was the dining room itself at the back of the house, a sitting room at the front, and upstairs were three bedrooms, a bathroom and a walk-in airing cupboard. The bedrooms in School House were small and full of furniture so there was never much room to move around, and they were only ever used for sleeping in. Our bathroom on the other hand was large, having been built in the first instance as a bedroom. It accommodated, as well as the three usual bathroom appointments, a large and a small chest of drawers, a chair, and a mahogany towel rail. The taps in bath and basin were brass, but as my mother was not keen on or had not the time to keep them polished she painted them with metallic gold paint, and when the tin of paint was left about my sister used it to paint her toenails. The bath, free-standing on fancy cast-iron feet, was also painted regularly – white of course, not metallic gold.

I remember the stairs from the cellar up to the hall inside the house being in use, but while I was still a child they were blocked off and a floor was put in to make a sewing cupboard for my mother. All our clothes were home-made, for my mother was a clever and creative dressmaker though entirely self taught. Only our underclothes, shoes and stockings were bought from the shops, and jerseys, socks and even our first swimming costumes were hand knitted. Material was readily available and cheap. The Mill manufactured the well-known Westmorland Tweed, and odd pieces at the end of a finished length were bought for a few shillings. Sometimes there was just a skirt length, sometimes enough for a coat, a dress or a suit. My father would come home from work with a piece of cloth under his arm, toss it over to my mother and say, "What about this? Five bob." She never refused it. Her sewing machine was a treadle model, and here in the sewing cupboard she worked often far into the night. She used to say that she liked to see us all off to bed – including my father – and then she could start her sewing.

There was no doubt about it that we were the best-dressed girls for miles around. Garments flowed thick and fast from her nimble and inventive fingers for my sister and me, and for our mother herself. As these clothes had cost so little to produce they could be embellished with expensive and unusual buttons and belts. When I look through my large tin of buttons and buckles, saved from many of these garments, a whole mannequin parade of colourful fashion passes before my mind's eye. Green circular buttons with tiny painted flowers from a princess-style dress; scarlet rectangles from a scarlet coat with green revers; brown wooden toggles from a beige suit; tiny green hearts from a party dress, and lovely gilt and inlaid buckles, some from hand-worked tapestry belts. The invitation for me to attend my first dance, for which a long dress was required, only gave twenty-four hours notice. My mother – and my maternal grandmother who by then was living with us – worked all day and almost all night to produce a dazzling multi-coloured taffeta gown with a completely separate under-skirt, frilled collar and jabot.

Cousins of my mother's who came to stay with us from West London were amazed by our village home, the hills surrounding it and by our North-Country accent which though not broad was nevertheless very different to theirs. They were given a tour of the Mill and took home with them several lengths of lovely woollen material. They called my father 'Lord Tweed', a nick-name which stuck for many years.

So here I grew up during the late nineteen-twenties and early thirties, in this mid-Victorian detached house with its gothic-revival-style church windows and fanlights, bounded on three side by garden and on the fourth by the village school. My mother, who had been a teacher before her marriage, was sometimes called upon to help in the school when one of the staff was ill, or as once happened when a teacher left and no immediate replacement had been found. On these occasions we went into school with her but were never regular pupils there. We were taught to read and write at home and neither of us started school until we were six years old, and then it was to attend the Kindergarten at Kendal High School as fee payers.

This set us apart somewhat, as all other village children attended the local school. We learned to take a few good-

natured jibes about our Kendal Green uniform, especially
our hats – cream straw Panamas in the summer, and green
velour hats with a brim in the winter. We had leather
satchels, hockey sticks, tennis raquets, music cases, and
above all, books. We took piano lessons and dancing
lessons, and if we were invited to parties we were sent and
brought home in a taxi. My father's wages certainly did not
pay for all this. He was a Foreman woollen-spinner at the
Mill and it was a reasonably good job. Many of the villagers
who worked there worked under him, but my mother had
a small private income, and she spent it lavishly and reck-
lessly on us.

Even though I was always aware that I had so much more
than the other children in Mealbank I did not want to be
treated differently by them. All I wanted was to be one of
them, and I think that because of this I was accepted as an
equal by most of them. My mother however showed no
signs of making a close friendship with any other women in
the village, though of course she would pass the time of day
very pleasantly with anyone she encountered. She was on
fairly intimate terms with my father's sisters, Sarah and
Mary, but she rarely sought their company or went to their
house, though they, and more particularly Auntie Mary,
spent a great deal of time pottering backwards and for-
wards between the two homes, gleaning snippets of news
and information and repeating what gossip they had picked
up from other sources. It must be said that my mother considered herself on a higher social level than that of her
neighbours and fellow villagers, as indeed I suppose she
was. Rather like the Squire's wife if there had been a Squire.
And from this it may be deduced that she was very much
the driving force in the household.

My father was a quiet, steady, kind and mild-mannered
man, slow to anger and with an impish sense of humour.
Who knows, perhaps he was quite happy to let my mother
take the reins, control the finances and make all the deci-
sions. She was certainly very capable of it. He was happy in
his garden and with his books. From the age of eleven he
had worked long hours at the Mill. The early death of his
father had meant that as many of the family as possible had

had to go out to work to provide the bare necessities of life. Luxuries there were none, and schooling was cut to the minimum. I believe his work tired him more than he ever admitted, and more than we ever knew. He was not a strong or robust man. About five feet eight inches tall and rather slightly built, he had green, almond-shaped eyes, and hair which was brown and curly when we were small, but which had become grey by the time I entered my teens.

He took no part – nor had any interest – in sporting activities, and apart from a weekly visit to the shops in Kendal on a Saturday and a week's holiday a year, usually at Morecambe, he rarely left the village. He had no desire to own a car, and even less desire to learn to drive one. In his own small way he was something of an artist. Some of the patterns he designed, which were woven into the materials he made at the Mill, went to the House of Dior in Paris. He wrote poetry, sadly none of which survived the family upheaval of the early 1960's, and great was his appreciation of everything in Nature. Surrounded by a family of women, wife, daughters, mother-in-law and sisters, he showed great forbearance, even if at times he was sorely tried.

When they married, my father was thirty-four years old and my mother twenty-five. An only child of doting parents, she came from a very different environment. Her father, a self-made man, ran a successful business and was comfortably off. Early presents from her parents included a fine gold bangle and a gold Rolex wrist watch. She went to grammar school and to train as a teacher. She was about five feet four inches tall and had a slim, erect figure. She was not beautiful, but her general appearance as a young woman was attractive. Her hair was what we called mousy, though we were assured that as a girl it had been the colour of ripe corn, and she had inherited her father's heavy-lidded eyes, though whereas his were bright blue hers were grey and gave her rather a melancholy countenance.

Her personality and her nature were exceedingly complex and volatile. She worked indefatigably in her house and

16

home; a good cook, a clever needle-woman, extravagant, creative, inventive, ambitious for us, she loved us fiercely and with a possessiveness which was at times frightening. She ruled us; not with a rod of iron, but she imposed her will on us to such an extent that long after I was married I was sometimes still afraid of her.

CHAPTER THREE

Westmorland Forebears

My paternal grandparents both came from North Westmorland farming families. Elizabeth Metcalfe, my grandmother, was born in 1854 at Bow Bridge, Asby, the eldest of the eight children of Nicholas and Elizabeth Metcalfe. The name of one of her brothers was Lancelot Fairer, Fairer being a common surname in that district. Lancelot was not an unusual name in Westmorland at that time and it was often shortened to Lanty. Less common, but in use locally was the Christian name Wolf, or sometimes Lupus, shortened to Lupe.

Uncle Lanty was a bachelor and lived in a tiny cottage in the Town Head area of Asby. Even though he died before I was born he was often spoken of with affection by my parents and by Aunties. I am grateful to be in possession of a large pewter dish and two pottery plates covered with a pattern of tiny red leaves which belonged to him.

John Robinson, my grandfather, was born in Howgill in 1855, the only son of Edmund and Anne Robinson of Marthwaite, Howgill, and of Hole House, Howgill. From the records it seems very probable that Edmund married a second time and produced two more sons and a daughter. John was baptised in Howgill Church shortly after it was built. Where he and Elizabeth set up home is not known for certain, but it was probably Draw Well in Howgill, and from here he went to work for the railway company in the coaling yard at Marthwaite. It was at Draw Well that their first five children were born, – Ann, Elizabeth, Sarah Agnes, Mary, and Edmund my father.

Draw Well is a small farm cottage sitting serenely in the midst of the Howgill fells on the land of the farm known as Bramaskew in the hamlet of Bland. The little house is a shrine for the Society of Friends, the Quakers, because in the seventeenth century George Fox visited it several times on his travels in that district. Its name is derived from the nearby well which never runs dry. It seems likely that John and

Elizabeth's remaining three children, the twins John and Fanny, and Hannah, were born at the Laurels, Scalthwaiterigg Stocks, though I can find no record of this.

The Laurels was a detached cottage, one of three dwellings standing together about two miles out of Kendal on the road to Appleby. It had only two bedrooms, and a small room at the back of the house which may have been an addition to the main building and which was used as a third bedroom. One cannot help wondering where all the children slept.

After moving from Howgill to Scalthwaiterigg John's employment changed. Perhaps it was this change which necessitated the move to the Laurels. A letter which has survived, written by him in December 1888 to his 'brother and sister' states:

"I was down at Kendal and Oxenholme today for my new clothes ... I have got quite used to box life now and the telegraph is no trouble to me, I can read it as well by ear as sight nearly."

This seems to indicate that he had gone to collect his new uniform and was now working in a signal box, possibly at Oxenholme which was an important and busy railway junction. Some months before this letter was written one of the twins, John, had died at the age of four months. Though he does not refer to this, he does write about the other twin, Fanny, how difficult she was to wean, and how she walked before she was a year old.

He and my grandmother and their large family were invited to a free charity Christmas dinner that year by the Mayor of Kendal, Mr Bindloss. But he informs us in a continuation of the letter to his brother and sister:

"I never stir far from home myself, my chief delight is in the Church and Sabbath School which I never fail to attend. I have put sin entirely behind my back and am travelling towards the heavenly Jerusalem."

We will never know what sin he had put entirely behind him, but we do know that the poor man, then only thirty-three years of age, was certainly on his way to "the heavenly Jerusalem." Five years later he died of lung cancer, the probable result of working in a coaling yard. "Little Hannah", as she was always called, followed him to the grave twelve months later at the age of four years.

My grandmother must have been an indomitable woman (it was said that she was up and about the day after giving birth) and here she was facing the future after losing two children and her husband in the space of five years.

So at the period of which I am writing, Granny Robinson, and Auntie Sally and Auntie Mary her daughters, lived near to School House in Woodside Terrace at the top end of the village. I first remember them when I was about three years old, and by then Aunties had long since given up working at the Mill and were living sedately and quietly and looking after their ailing mother.

Granny was always dressed in black, with a skirt which almost reached her ankles, black stockings and shoes. She rarely went out and always seemed to be sitting on the sofa facing the window. I was a little afraid of her because she complained if we were noisy, in fact she seemed to complain all the time. This may well have provoked my sister, having been rebuked by her, into saying, "Not 'ike Garny best, 'ike Auntie Mamy best". This no doubt secretly pleased Auntie Mary but robbed Granny of any remaining patience she had with the child. This incident probably took place before I was born, but it was in Aunties' repertoire of tales and sayings which they related from time to time.

I did not realise then of course that Granny was not very well, and when I was six years old she died at the age of seventy-seven. My second cousin from Howgill provides the following tale. Granny Robinson lay dying, and her family were assembled round her bed so that she could see them for the last time on Earth. She fell asleep and they felt that the end was imminent. However, Granny opened her eyes, looked around at her son and her daughters and said in her rather humourless and matter-of-fact voice, "You're all still here, I haven't gone yet then."

After her death the two Aunties kept house together. Auntie Sally was the older sister. Her real name was Sarah Agnes; her sisters called her Sarah but to us she was Auntie Sally. She was a tiny person, barely five feet tall. Her body was thin and frail, and her legs so skeletal one marvelled how they supported her. Her face was small and her features neat and regular, and her whole expression serious, kind, somewhat sanctimonious and rather soulful, partly because of her deep set, heavy-lidded grey eyes. Her grey and rather crispy hair was drawn back into a little bun as was the fashion of the time. All her movements were slow and steady and she was never known to hurry.

As girls we were all agog to hear of any romance there might have been in the lives of our Aunts, and we were led to believe that Auntie Sally had once had a boy friend. He emigrated to Canada to become a farmer and had wanted her to go with him. The enormity of this step was much more than she felt she could undertake, and so he went alone and she stayed at home and remained unmarried. How unadventurous we thought. And so her life revolved around the Wesleyan and Methodist chapels, the Band of Hope, and the household in which she lived, never moving far from home. We know that she visited her two older sisters, Annie in Lancaster and Lizzie in Cross Flatts, and occasionally went on the bus to see a cousin Maggie who lived in Appleby, but these visits were few and far between. Her lack of strength was obvious. She could barely lift a pan from the fire, and sat down with a mixing bowl between her knees to beat the butter, sugar and eggs for a cake. She undertook no strenuous or heavy household work, and thus preserved what strength she had to live to be eighty years old.

Auntie Mary was two years younger and a perfect foil to her sister. She was a First World War widow and from photographs taken in her teens and early womanhood had been very beautiful. Taller than Auntie Sally but still only slightly built she was erect and a quick mover. Her hair, which had been thick, brown and curly, but which was now grey, still retained some ringlets which fell onto her forehead. Her eyes were green, almond-shaped, bright and twinkling, and her mouth was forever turned up at the corners for she was always laughing.

She had married Tom Blenkhorn in August 1911 when she was twenty-nine years old. He lived with his parents, sisters and brothers in School House, where we now lived. Tom and Mary both worked at the Mill and this was how they met, became acquainted, and fell in love. Very little is known of this period, but what is known is that the Blenkhorn family moved to Colne in Lancashire round about 1905 and either set up or took over a laundry business there. Picture postcards have survived which were sent by Auntie Mary to her mother and sisters on her visits to Colne in 1905 and 1906. So it was a long courtship. Nothing unusual about that in those days however, and it was to Colne that Auntie Mary went as a bride after the wedding at Skelsmergh Church. Picture postcards again give us an all-too-brief glimpse of the early days in Colne. On August 11, 1911 a card was posted in Colne to Auntie Sally:

"Dear Sarah, I find I can't get the hat pins packed have about half a dozen boxes and none of them will do of course they will stick out of the paper will send them later. Would you let me have my hat for Sunday please."

And on August 25, 1911 another card was sent from Cleveland Street, Colne by Auntie Mary to her mother:

"Dear Mother, Thanks very much for the hats received at dinner time safe and sound one of the men from the laundry brought it for me from the station. Will you let me know when the pots are coming. I am nothing but a bother. Hope you are quite well.
Your loving D. Mary."

Some more punctuation marks would have helped the reader.

Their first home was the little terraced house of 44 Cleveland Street, built around 1880 or 1890, so by no means an old house when they took up residence. Quite soon they moved to 9 Langroyd Road, Colne. This house was of similar vintage, an end-of-terrace house with a bay window, altogether more spacious and in a better locality.

Uncle Tom Blenkhorn worked in the family laundry business. Auntie Mary may well have worked there too because picture postcards from her mention being at work, and "the laundry girls". One card to Auntie Sally is undated, has no postmark, probably having been sent in an envelope, and reads, referring to the picture on the card:

"Dear Sarah, How do you like this one isn't it lovely. Have been thinking about you today at work. It was eleven o'clock or near when we arrived here last night. I was tired. It is a lovely place. Tom has just gone for a shave, so am all alone (enjoying ourselves)."

Are they away somewhere, having travelled in the evening after work? Was the card started one day and finished the following day? It is difficult to decide, and unfortunately I shall never know just where they went.

I try to picture Auntie Mary in her new situation in Colne; a small busy town in Lancashire so very different from the quiet rural surroundings in which she had been brought up. Her circumstances too were considerably altered. In her mother's home there would only be money for the necessities; but her husband was the part-owner of a thriving business, and had filled their new home with tasteful and high quality furniture.

I do not know exactly when Uncle Tom was called up after the outbreak of war in 1914. Conscription for single men was introduced in January 1916 and for married men in May 1916. What I have been told is that he desperately did not want to join up, and the night before his Army medical examination he and a friend apparently "went into a cellar to clean some old beds", and inhaled as much of the dusty atmosphere as they could in the hope of failing the medical.

Alas for them. They passed the examination "A1" and Uncle Tom was drafted into the King's Liverpool Regiment and sent to France. As soon as he had gone, and I do not know at what stage of the War this was – though I can assume that it was some time after May 1916 – Auntie Mary put her furniture into store and returned to her mother's home at Scalthwaiterigg Stocks. I have to say that I find this extraordinary. Surely she should have kept the home intact hopeful for his return, as thousands of other wives did? Perhaps if there had been children she would have done so. But there were those who said that she should never have married at all because she was "too much of a home bird".

She returned home to her mother and brother and two of her sisters. Before her re-entry into her mother's household, Auntie Fanny and my father, Ted, would be the breadwinners of the family. Auntie Mary would have her Army allowance with which to make her contribution to the household budget, but Auntie Sally probably did not go out to work. It was not long, however, before circumstances caused changes to this new arrangement. In March 1918 Uncle Tom Blenkhorn was killed in one of the battles of the Somme. He has no known grave but is commemorated on a memorial in Ham British Cemetery in France. His name also appears on the 1914-1918 War Memorial in Colne, and on that in Skelsmergh Church. On July 23rd of that same year, 1918, Auntie Fanny married Tom Hackett, and they set up home in Kendal. In the following April, 1919, my father married my mother. These events meant the loss of two regular incomes in my grandmother's household, and it seems very much as though Auntie Mary's War Widow's pension was the mainstay of the home. After Uncle Tom Blenkhorn's death their furniture came out of store. Much of it furnished the little house in Woodside Terrace in Mealbank to which Granny and her daughters moved in the early 1920's. The elegant Art Nouveau dining suite came to my parents at School House.

There was never any spoken or whispered suggestion of any other man in Auntie Mary's life. As I grew into my teens I often wondered how it was she had never remarried. So many War Widows did marry again, and there is no doubt that she was lovely to look at and a capable housewife. But on reflection many years later I realised that she had no desire for another marriage. Her late husband was remembered, thought of and spoken of with a deep and loving reverence, and no one could have taken his place. It seemed as though a quiet and uneventful life with her old mother and delicate sister was enough for her. They settled down in the cottage in Woodside Terrace, near to our family, near to the Chapel, surrounded by neighbours, and in such a small village they would soon become integrated into it and a very much respected part of it.

CHAPTER FOUR

Aunties' House

The front door of Aunties' house in Woodside Terrace was approached through a wooden gate and along a a short pebbled path with a rock garden on one side. The door opened straight into the living-room. Here on the thick and softly coloured carpet, which rose and fell on the undulating stone-flagged floor, were the old gate-legged table, the dresser with the plate rack above, the ladder-backed rocking chair with deep-buttoned cushions in moss green velvet, and the mahogany glass-fronted bookcase and cupboard, full of pink and white cups and saucers and ornate teapots, side by side with *Pilgrim's Progress*, *Windyridge* and *Jane Eyre*.

The focal point of the room was the hearth, with its open fire of coal and wood and the kitchen range, black-leaded and polished until it shone. Here all the cooking was done. Even though electricity was installed on the ground floor for lighting late in the 1930's, it was not until after the Second World War that Aunties indulged in such luxuries as an electric kettle and a boiling ring.

The kitchen, which contained a small brown sink with a cold tap under the window, a working table and a pantry, was more of a wide passageway to the staircase than a room, and in this passageway was housed the harmonium. It was a lovely little French instrument on which Auntie Sally played – slowly and gently – the softer and often more mournful hymns from The Methodist Hymn Book, and on which I, once I had learned to read music, thundered out the noisiest and most boisterous hymns I could find. It was from Auntie Sally that I first learned that hymn tunes all had a name and a metre. Cwm Rhondda was one of my favourites, and Lyngham to which we sang "O for a thousand tongues to sing". Auntie Mary rarely got beyond "O for a thou-hou-hou-hou-hou-sand" before collapsing with laughter in her chair. Auntie Sally was slightly disapproving but could not resist a smile.

Aunties sang, on and off, for much of the day. Auntie Mary sang as she went about her daily tasks. First World War songs, especially "There is a Tavern in the Town", and "It's a long way to Tipperary", featured prominently in her repertoire along with "Genevieve", "I'll take you home again, Kathleen" (Auntie Sally joined in with these), and "I dreamt that I dwelt in marble halls". All this singing was unaccompanied as there was no sheet music. I have wondered where my Aunts learned these popular songs of the day. There was no radio and they had never been to the cinema. Perhaps they went with their friends to amateur concerts or sing-songs in Kendal.

So at a very early age I unconsciously committed to memory the words and music of a great many songs and hymns, and hardly a day passed without my playing a tune on the harmonium, standing in its rather incongruous position in the little kitchen passageway.

The spiral stairs, with their shining brass stair-rods, led to a large front bedroom where Aunties shared a big brass bedstead and feather bed. They were quite accustomed to sharing a bed, as I have remarked earlier one wonders where and how all the family slept at The Laurels; certainly a year or two after the turn of the century when the two oldest daughters, Ann and Elizabeth had married and left home, and when Tom Metcalfe had come to live there, Tom slept in the little room at the back of the house, my father had one of the bedrooms, and in the other bedroom Granny and Auntie Fanny shared one bed, and Auntie Mary and Auntie Sally shared another bed. Ann's daughter Edith first came to stay at the cottage from Lancaster when she was four years old, in 1909, travelling alone on the train in the Guard's Van (looked after by the guard who gave her a penny). Telling me of the sleeping arrangements at The Laurels she said, "Oh, I just slept among them". So after Auntie Mary's return to her mother's home, and the removal to Woodside Terrace, it would be the most natural thing for the sisters to share a bed as they had done from their childhood to being young women.

The most imposing item of furniture in Aunties' bedroom was a large oak roll-topped desk which had belonged to Uncle Tom Blenkhorn. I feel sure that it would have come from the offices of the Laundry. Having seen the two houses where Aunty Mary and Uncle Tom lived in Colne I cannot imagine it being in either, apart from the fact that it was of very little use as a domestic piece of furniture. It was little used in this bedroom. The pigeon holes and tiny drawers under the roll top were empty, and the small drawers on either side of the knee-hole held only gloves and scarves. Almost the only other memento belonging to Uncle Tom was a small crimson leather dressing-case, in pristine condition, containing silver toilet requisites, and this we liked to look at and to take out very carefully, – the soap box, the toothbrush holder, and other cylindrical containers for mysterious lotions.

There was a smaller bedroom at the back of the house with a text on the wall, "Be thou faithful" and on the chest of drawers a lovely Moorcroft bowl and a little book of verses called *Bees in Amber.*

A door opened onto a second flight of stairs, uncarpeted but scrubbed almost white, which led to the attic. Stepping into the attic from the stairs one faced the window. The windowsill was low and wide and made an ideal window seat, and sitting here one looked out onto fields which rose steeply and where there were always cows grazing. These beasts were said to be forecasters of the weather. When they sat down in the bottom of the field it would be wet, when they climbed the hill and ate the grass it would be fine.

To the left-hand side of the attic was a big pine chest of drawers, and it was this chest which held the treasures we had come up to see. With great care and reverence Auntie Mary took from one of the drawers Uncle Tom Blenkhorn's medals and their ribbons and the bundles of his letters written to her from France, tied up with blue ribbon. The ribbon around the letters was never untied so their contents were never revealed. Then came the wreath of artificial orange blossom worn on her wedding day, and her wedding photographs. We gazed with awe on these rather pathetic little mementoes, not aware of the heartbreak and heartache which they must have evoked.

Then there was the album of picture postcards, many of them even then thirty to forty years old. This was Auntie Sally's collection and most of the cards had been sent to her. There were famous female celebrities of the day, others depicting hymns – wild scenes for "Rock of Ages" and "Lead Kindly Light" – and there was one postcard which opened like a book and had a pink paper rose inside.

The clothes closet behind the partition to the right of the stair-rail was also a delight, and if we were on our best behaviour we were allowed to open up the old round hat boxes. If it was summer time the boxes would be full of hats put away until winter, and of fur neckties, complete with head, tail and paws. We would stroke the nose and paws and then prance around the attic wearing the fur. If it was winter time the summer hats would be in the boxes, shiny black, wide brimmed, and straw creations decorated with bunches of cherries and all manner of artificial flowers. The crowning moment of the visit to the attic was to have a drop of "Rapture" behind the ears. This perfume was in a small wide cut-glass bottle with a narrow neck, and Auntie Mary carefully dabbed a little behind each of our ears. How we dodged having to be washed after this touch of "Rapture".

This little house was my second home. Indeed in school holidays I think that I spent more time in it than in my own home. My mother was always cooking, baking, washing, cleaning, sewing, gardening, painting, papering or doing any of the hundred-and-one jobs with which she filled her day to capacity – and all of which she executed so well that I often ran to Aunties where life was taken at a much more leisurely pace, and where we would sit out in the sun, or inside over the fire, and they would dreamily reminisce and tell me stories of their own girlhood, stories I never tired of hearing.

If I stayed until after tea on a winter's evening, the oil lamp would be lit and the thick paper blind drawn down over the window. I pulled the rocking chair up to the fire and per-suaded Auntie Mary to make me a raw onion sandwich with plenty of salt on it. Then the time came, perhaps at about seven o'clock, for me to be taken home. But first the lantern had to be lit. The lantern was made of tin, it was octagonal with glass sides and it was lit by a candle in the middle and held by a big metal ring at the top. This was a very necessary piece of equipment as there were no street lights at the top end of the village, and its metal frame and glass sides threw interesting and sometimes rather frightening shadows onto the uneven road. Electric torches did not enter Aunties' lives until many years later, and even then the lantern never went out of service. It lighted our way between Woodside Terrace and School House for as long as I can remember.

The slow pace of Aunties' lives did not mean that they were lazy or slovenly. Quite the reverse; they were scrupulously clean, neat, spick and span, and kept house on a very small income. Auntie Mary had only her First World War widow's pension, and a small amount of capital which she had inherited from her husband. Auntie Sally had no income at all until single women were provided for by the State, and then it was a meagre amount; so Auntie Mary's £2 a week kept them both. The rent for their house was four shillings and elevenpence a week, and every Monday morning two half-crowns were put with the rent book on the old gate-legged table under the window and were collected by a clerk from the Mill, leaving them, of course, a penny change.

Pennies, halfpennies and even farthings, for they were legal tender for a time, were important. With a penny stamp one could post a letter. A penny would buy a picture post-card which only needed a ha'penny stamp on it. Twopence would buy a packet of note paper and envelopes. A ball of string, a box of matches, a pencil, or a box of drawing pins all could be bought for a penny. So too could a bottle of ink, a pair of shoelaces, a pen and nib (the long thin scratchy sort), a paint brush for water colours and an unending list of items of sweets and confectionery.

The youngest sister, Auntie Fanny, cycled up to the village from Kendal – which was about three miles away – two or three times a week, and often brought shopping, little bags of this and that. There was always a great financial reckoning over what had been spent and what had to be paid back, down to the very last farthing. In the winter, when she had to ride home to Kendal in the dark, her cycle lamp had to be lit. It was a large ornate lamp. The lower half of it contained carbide which looked like lumps of chopped-up chalk, and the top half of the lamp was filled with water which dripped slowly onto the carbide. This action produced a strong smelling gas which was lit with a match. The light it produced was white and clear, and on one side of the lamp was a little green cut glass and on the other side a red glass and these glowed green and red when the lamp was lit. And so Auntie Fanny slotted the lamp onto the bracket at the front of the bicycle and set off through the wood to ride the three miles home to Kendal.

Aunties' fire was lit every day whatever the weather, indeed it had to be to boil the kettle and cook the food, so it was important that the lighting of the fire should be as free from difficulties as possible. Firelighters were made from rolled up sheets of newspaper. Aunties did not take a daily or a Sunday paper, but Auntie Fanny – who took morning, evening and weekend papers – kept them supplied. A whole sheet of paper was spread out on the floor and rolled tightly from corner to corner with the palm of the hand. It took a fair amount of practice for a child to acquire this skill. When the paper had been completely rolled into a long tight cylinder it was wound round the hand and the end was tucked through the middle and left sticking out. This was the bit that was lit when two or three firelighters had been placed in the grate. Sticks and coal were quickly put on top and away the fire went.

The kitchen range comprised of an oven on the left-hand side, a water jacket on the right, and the fire in the middle. There was a moveable plate or bar on which to stand the pans so that they could be directly over the heat or as far from it as required. The kettle hung from a reckan, which in turn was suspended from the chimney crane. On days when the oven was to be used, and this was often, the cover was removed from the hole in the side under the oven and the fire was stoked up and sent roaring into the hole to heat up the oven.

Auntie Fanny's husband, Uncle Tom Hackett, was Works Manager at the Mill, and on five days a week he came to Aunties for his mid-day dinner. This entailed long and slow preparations which took all morning, starting as soon as the breakfast of bread and honey had been cleared away and washed up.

Uncle Tom was a great favourite of mine, partly no doubt because he was the only uncle who lived near us, and partly because he was full of fun and always willing, indeed keen, to play any kind of games, – card games, board games or ball games. He came for his dinner at twelve o'clock, and as my father did not come for his dinner until half-past twelve I could very often sit and watch Uncle Tom eat. It was always very much the same kind of meal: meat and potatoes in some form. Cold meat cut from the joint on Monday, hot-pot or hash on Tuesday and Wednesday, meat and potato pie with a pie crust, sometimes a jacket potato, sometimes beef and ham roll. Except for onions, vegetables did not feature in Aunties' menus. Puddings however most certainly did. Creamy rice pudding in a tall brown pot was put into the oven soon after nine o'clock to be ready for mid-day. Sometimes it was rough tapioca, and on special occasions it was big sago, or bullet sago as Auntie Sally called it. Uncle Tom always did justice to his meal, and so as not to leave a trace of gravy he very often lifted up his plate and licked it clean. A compliment to the cooks you might say. Having observed this procedure several times I suggested to my mother at our own dinner table that I might "lick my plate like my Uncle Tom", to which she replied sharply, "I shall whip you if you do."

Auntie Mary did the baking. She rolled out her pastry on a big tin tray on the kitchen table to make 'blobby' cracknels. How we loved to eat hot the ones with the biggest blobs in them. There were Queen cakes and Feather cakes mixed by Auntie Sally, sitting in front of the fire with the basin

33

between her knees. There were Shrewsbury biscuits, currant pasty and golden sticky gingerbread. These delights appeared on doylies in pretty china dishes or glass cake stands on the tea table. All the bread was home-made; white, brown, teacakes, and nut bread at Christmas. The trays of bread and teacakes were laid in the hearth to rise. One day at such a time we rushed in with Glen, our Cairn terrier, who smelled the bread and licked the teacakes all over. Mercifully both Aunties were in the kitchen at the time

Potatoes were cooked in iron pans on the fire and jam was made over the fire too. Auntie Mary made toffee: Everton, treacle, and sometimes fudge, and all too often when she was telling us a tale she would forget the toffee and it would boil over and run down the sides of the pan into the fire. How she laughed, and how Auntie Sally gently remonstrated.

In a silk-lined case there was a set of half-a-dozen tea-knives which appeared on the tea table on Sundays. These were the only stainless steel knives in the house. The every-day cutlery consisted of knives with cylindrical, unpolished brown wooden handles and ordinary steel blades, and matching forks with only three prongs. The blades of kitchen, carving and table knives were cleaned by rubbing them vigorously with a damp cork dipped in Vim.

Aunties had very small appetites, in fact my mother once remarked that they "ate like birds". Much of their cooking and baking was done to feed others, for as well as having Uncle Tom to dinner on five days a week they entertained countless friends to tea. In those days you were invited out to tea, never to dinner – which was the main meal and always taken in the middle of the day. In our world no one ate dinner in the evening. That was only for sections of society one read about either in books or in the newspapers. Tea at Aunties was Afternoon Tea: bread and butter with jam, buttered tea-cakes, scones, and a variety of cakes and pastries with occasionally toast, made at the fire, but that was rather special.

None of the Aunties made their own dresses – indeed they all marvelled at my mother's expertise as a needle-woman – but in the attic there was an old treadle sewing machine, so someone at sometime must have been able to sew. However they all knitted socks, but they either could not or would not follow a knitting pattern for any other kind of garment. Socks were knitted without a pattern and without ceasing, thus my father and Uncle Tom were always kept supplied. Aunties' other occupation in the field of what would now be called Cottage Crafts was the making of "peggy" rugs. A piece of clean sacking was cut to the required size and the edges turned in. A simple design was drawn onto it. Discarded woollen or tweed garments were cut into small strips. Then with a smoothly polished piece of wood about the size of a large pencil and pointed at one end, holes were made in the sacking and the strips of material pushed down through one hole and up again through another, following the pattern with different colours of material. These rugs were used in the kitchen. They were thick, warm and colourful and lasted for ages.

CHAPTER FIVE

35 Castle Garth

Auntie Fanny has already been briefly mentioned. She was the youngest surviving member of the family. The youngest, Hannah, had died at the age of four years. Auntie Fanny was a twin, and her twin brother John had lived for only four months. She had married Thomas Hackett of Kendal after a courtship of seven years, during which time they had saved up the necessary three hundred and seventy-five pounds to buy a small terrace house in Castle Garth, Kendal. To us as teenagers during the Second World War, when engagements were brief and sometimes non-existent, a seven-year courtship seemed unimaginably ludicrous; but long engagements were normal during the period between the Wars, and indeed – for couples wanting to buy their own house who would never contemplate borrowing money to do so – there was no alternative but to wait until the necessary sum had been saved.

And so Auntie Fanny and Uncle Tom were married on 23 July 1918, and after a honeymoon at Hawkshead they took up residence at 35 Castle Garth. The two-storey house was next-but-one to the end of the terrace near to the approach to Castle Hill, and it was a quiet and highly respectable area. The front of the house with a downstairs bay window and tiny garden faced onto the road. The backs of the houses were approached by a wide back lane with an un-made-up road. There was no access from front to back along the length of the terrace, except of course through the houses. At the back of the house there was a good-sized yard with a very small patch of garden, an outside WC, a coal house and a wash house.

The interior of the house was a show-piece. My Aunt and Uncle had no children so perhaps Auntie Fanny put all her energy and interest into the house. Devoid of great intellect or cultural pursuits her life revolved around keeping house, visiting her sisters and her friends, and the Chapel and its activities. Enough you may say to keep her fully occupied. I am quite sure she never yearned for anything else, unless it was to regret not having produced any children. The cleanliness in the house was breathtaking. Not a speck of dust was to be seen anywhere and not a thing was out of place. A new bathroom was installed in the mid-1930's. Its design was what would now be described as pure Art Deco. Yellow marbled panelling, yellow bath and basin with black trimmings and chromium-plated edging to all the fitments. It was rather incongruous in relation to the old-fashioned-style furnishings and decorations of the rest of the house.

The front sitting room was hardly ever used except on Christmas Day, but occasionally I was allowed to play the piano – very much out of tune and therefore not an attractive proposition for long – and to look at, but not sit on, a tiny gilt chair. All the rooms were crammed with furniture, and in the dining room there was just sufficient space to walk between the table and its four dining chairs in the centre of the room, and the sideboard, settee, bureau, two easy chairs and cabinet containing the wireless set. The table was the centrepiece of the room. It was large, oval, and polished to a mirror-like finish, and on which we were not allowed to lay a finger. Before a meal was set onto this table it was first covered with a thick felt, then a pristine damask cloth, and finally cork place-mats with black-and-orange-beaded edges.

My Aunt and Uncle used this room for sitting and relaxation, that is to say if Auntie Fanny could ever be said to relax. I don't think she ever read, she may have glanced at the newspapers or a magazine (*Home Chat* and *People's Friend*) but she knitted socks and popped in and out of her neighbours and sometimes trotted off to a Chapel function.

It sounds a dull and harsh regime, and perhaps not the sort of place or the kind of people that a child would want to visit regularly. But that was not the case at all. We loved our Aunt and Uncle and they loved us as though we were their own children. Auntie Fanny was my godmother, and maybe because of that I was her favourite. Not only did I see her on the two or three days a week when she visited Aunties at Mealbank, but as children Zelia and I went to tea at Castle Garth every Saturday afternoon, and after a scrumptious afternoon tea we played card games and Bagatelle; not, I may say, on the sacred dining table but on a green-baize-topped card table. Playing Bridge was a serious social activity (not for Auntie Fanny it must be said, though of course she had to enter into it), and they frequently entertained and were entertained by Bridge-playing friends and in-laws.

Uncle Tom was as keen as mustard on games of every description. He had played football for Kendal in his youth, and followed closely his home team of Netherfield. After he returned from the Saturday afternoon game, and the football match results were read out on the wireless after tea, he entered them all in his local evening paper to pore over later on. It must have been rather disappointing for him not having anyone with whom he could discuss sport, but, like my father, he was surrounded by women, – wife, sisters-in-law and nieces. As a young man he had apparently enjoyed a glass of beer, just how much beer we never knew, but Auntie Fanny used to say that she would not have married him unless he had given up drinking. I never heard of or saw him drink alcohol of any kind at any time, so he must have taken her at her word.

At the age of fifty-nine he had a severe nervous breakdown, and it became clear after some months that retirement from work was the only way he would regain his health. This imposed a great financial strain on the household. It was not fully explained to me at the time, but I gathered that Uncle Tom had refused to fill in a Means Test form and so forfeited his right to a full pension. What he apparently received was three pounds a week, and Auntie Fanny had to manage on this. He gave up smoking his pipe and meals became less lavish. But he did recover his health and his good spirits, and he and Auntie Fanny cycled out two or three times a week, sometimes to Sandside or Arnside and along the country lanes to small villages they knew. On the days when they didn't cycle out together he walked about ten miles a day and she came to visit her sisters. This was a time in their lives which they enjoyed to the full. The sun and fresh air gave them a permanently golden-brown complexion, and their hands (for they never wore gloves) were the colour of Autumn leaves. I could not help noticing the contrast with my own parents. My father, pale, grey and tired-looking, working all day in that noisy, dreadful mill. How he must have longed to retire; but my mother's ever hungry need for money kept him at work for far too long.

CHAPTER SIX

Chapel and Church

The "Glory Hole" was a walk-in cupboard under the stairs of the little house in Woodside Terrace. In it were kept – as well as firelighters, sticks and buckets of coal – all the cleaning materials: Zebo black lead for the fireplace, and linseed oil and Mansion polish for the furniture. There was a long, soft sweeping brush and a coarser hand brush and dustpan which were used to brush the carpets. No electric vacuum cleaner of course, not even a Ewbank to take up the crumbs. In the deeper recesses of the Glory Hole were the glue-pot and a box with a few basic tools in it, a hammer, screwdriver, a pricker, old scissors and a few nails and screws, though I don't remember ever seeing Aunties wielding any of these implements. A canvas bag full of dusters and polishing cloths hung from a hook on the wall, and from another hook hung Aunties' dust caps, made of cotton, – these resembled a modern shower cap and covered the hair and ears and were donned on Fridays when the big cleaning operations took place.

The ashes and cinders from the fire fell into a deep pit under the grate and this "Big Hole", as it was called, had to be emptied once a week on a Friday. Auntie Mary would get down on her knees in a big sacking apron, wearing her dust cap, with her sleeves rolled up as far as they would go, and delve into the Big Hole with a small shallow tin, bringing it up full of ashes to empty into a bucket. After the Big Hole was emptied the brass knobs on the Tidy and the brass tap on the water jacket were polished. Then the whole kitchen range was black-leaded with Zebo, including the chimney crane and the reckan. The steps outside the front door were scrubbed, and the edges decorated with cream-coloured step stones which could be bought in several shades from white to a deep mustard colour.

Thus the big cleaning jobs were done ready for the weekend, for Sunday was a Day of Rest, and woe betide us if we produced a game of Snakes and Ladders or Ludo or dominoes on that day. Even knitting and sewing were banned in Aunties' house on Sundays. Reading however was allowed providing one did not overstep the limit and produce a comic. Auntie Sally read *The Christian Herald* and excerpts from *Pilgrim's Progress*. Auntie Mary would don her gold-rimmed pince-nez and read to me from *Anne of Green Gables* or *Little Women*. I would have preferred *Jane Eyre* but this was considered unsuitable for Sunday. Had I been sufficiently interested there might have been a chapter from *The Lonely Plough* by Constance Holme, whose books held Aunties in thrall but which I found, having tried the first chapters, unutterably dull and 'old fashioned'. It would be many years before my opinions underwent a radical change.

The Sunday Chapel service was held in the village school-room in the afternoon. It was undoubtedly the highlight of Aunties' week. Sometimes an ordained minister took the service, sometimes it was a local preacher, but one always knew well in advance who would be in charge because of "The Plan". This pamphlet was issued once a quarter and gave the names of those preaching on each Sunday at each chapel service in the circuit. Aunties took it in turns with two other sisters living together in the village to entertain the preacher to tea after the service, so when the Plan arrived we hastily scanned it to see who was destined to visit Woodside Terrace. What bliss if we were lucky enough to be able to invite my favourite young parsons! What abysmal tragedy if they were scheduled to go to the rivals' camp. Not all the names we read out from the Plan were greeted with enthusiasm however, even by Aunties. Mr So-and-So was condemned as 'a ranter', and Mr Bloggs was so severe and prim that conversation with him on any topic other than religion was out of the question. I kept away from Woodside Terrace when these gentlemen came to tea.

The service was attended by only a handful of people, a dozen at the most, and all women. It simply did not occur to me then that none of these women, including my two Aunties, had a man, neither father, brother nor husband;

they were all either single or widowed. The Christian religion in the form of Methodism, and more precisely in the shape of the Minister, took the place of a man in their lives. These men were put on a pedestal and became objects of reverence, admiration and adulation. They could do and say no wrong.

Uncle Tom had less laudatory opinions of the Methodist clergy however, and had no hesitation in expressing his views loudly, often in front of his wife – who was also a chapel-goer though rather less intense than her sisters – and in front of these two Aunts, whose distress, though evident, was commendably silent. Uncle Tom attended neither Church nor Chapel, but was apparently not averse to leaning back in his armchair on occasions and singing boisterously in a quite pleasing Baritone, "Shall we gather at the river?" and, "What a friend we have in Jesus", neither did it offend any Christian principles he may have had to take the name of the Lord in vain. Auntie Fanny, though a good cook and excellent housekeeper, was not blessed with intellect and many was the time that Uncle Tom, having become exasperated by her often foolish remarks, would exclaim, "Oh Christ, Fanny!" The occasional swear word also passed his lips, usually *sotto voce*. All this was anathema to the three Aunts but very exciting to us, especially as I had once been sent to bed for the afternoon for saying 'damn'. And being sent to bed meant having to change into pyjamas and get into bed and have the curtains drawn. In the middle of a sunny afternoon, to be imprisoned and humiliated thus was bad enough, but to hear from the darkened bedroom the shouts and the laughter from my friends playing out side was unbearable.

So then, the Sunday afternoon service took place in the schoolroom. The school was divided into two rooms by a folding partition, the top half of which was glass. Having originally been built as a chapel it was lofty, stark and bare and extremely difficult to heat. The congregation sat on immensely thick wooden benches, and the preacher stood at a small table in front of, and facing them. Music for the hymns was provided by a large American organ, long since past its best, and it was played and pedalled with great gusto by a lady known to everyone as Auntie Bessie. She swayed on her stool, as she not only played and pedalled but sang lustily as well. What was perhaps lacking in robes, flowers, ornaments and stained glass was made up for by the singing, and, "Stand up, stand up for Jesus" and, "Tell me the old, old story" could be heard quite clearly outside and roundabout.

Aunties' admiration of the Ministers had understandably rubbed off onto me. On these High Days, when the young minister came to tea, he and I would make the toast kneeling in front of the fire, with the brasses winking and the black leading shining; slice after slice of Auntie Mary's home-made bread we toasted on the end of hand-made wire toasting forks. Sometimes, before tea, we would ride off in his little Morris 8 to another outlying village to bring a young colleague who, apparently, had not been invited out to tea, and the three of us would make the toast, and they would gently tease me, and I thought that I was surely in Seventh Heaven.

One day, a year or so after these tea-parties, when I had become less of an ingenuous child and had acquired the first smattering of poise as a teenager, I was cycling home from Kendal wearing a new wine-coloured corded velvet suit, and a pale hyacinth-blue scarf tied at a fashionable angle – feeling in no doubt about how attractive I looked – when I met my favourite, driving towards Kendal. He stopped and we chatted. What a drop into the Pit for me to be told, carefully and tactfully, that he was soon to be married. What misery for a fourteen-year-old to endure!

The Chapel had its special occasions of course when almost all the village turned out to attend. The Flower Service in June, when the long table was massed with wild and garden blooms, and the fragrance filled the schoolroom. Each child, carrying a posy, either sang a song or recited a poem, and we sang, "Summer suns are glowing" and, "All things bright and beautiful", and Aunties wore their silk dresses with lace at the throat, and sewed flowers onto their straw hats.

CHAPEL AND CHURCH

The Harvest Festival in the Autumn was even more popular, and brought the whole village out regardless of
denomination. The Thanksgiving Service was followed by
an auction sale of the produce which had been given. Fruit,
flowers, vegetables, home-made jam, chutney and pickles,
bread and cakes, and some, but not many, tinned goods. The
sale was conducted by a farmer who was also a local
preacher; a towering figure with wild, auburn hair and an
enormous waxed moustache – his voice matched his stature
and could be heard half-way round the village. In those
days, and especially in a country district, tinned foods were
something of a novelty. Our auctioneer had obviously never
seen or heard of one commodity when he held up a tin of
spaghetti and bellowed, "What 'ave we 'ere then? Tinned
spag-et."

The Anglican Church was in the adjoining parish of
Skelsmergh, and was about a mile-and-a-half from
Mealbank. My parents were not regular attenders at either
church or chapel, and neither were we urged to attend.
However, some of my school friends who lived in
Skelsmergh Parish went to church and it wasn't long before
I joined them. For a time I attended both church and chapel,
but I soon found the church services more to my liking and
gave up chapel-going. Aunties were, of course, disappoint-
ed, and slightly disapproving, as in their opinion this was
the road to Popery.

It was, in fact, very 'low' church. But the church building,
simple and bare by any standards, nevertheless provided
surroundings and an atmosphere which appealed to me.
The stained glass, the ornaments, flowers, the music, and
above all the dignity and discipline of the ritual and the
incomparable language of the King James Bible and the
Book of Common Prayer, together with the professionalism
of the Anglican clergy, wooed me away from the harshness
and the extempore pulpit-thumping of largely untrained
preachers in the Methodist chapel.

The church of St John the Baptist in the parish of
Skelsmergh stood on a hill, looking east towards Mealbank
and Benson Knott, north towards Selside, south over

Kendal and west towards Burneside and the Lakeland hills. It was an exposed and rather bleak situation and the west door received the full force of the prevailing south-westerly winds. Entry to the churchyard was through an attractive lych-gate where stood the War Memorial, and on its wooden cross – along with other names of men from the Parish who had given their lives – was a brass plate bearing the name of Thomas Blenkhorn, Auntie Mary's husband.

The short walk from the lych-gate to the west door on a cold and wet blustery day could be devastating to clothes and hair-dos, especially, as often happened, if one had to struggle with the massive iron door handle. It could also be a distressing experience – as over the years I was to learn only too well – for a funeral procession walking slowly in a tearing wind. Many years later an inspired alteration was made. The west door was removed and the lower third of the ensuing space was built up in limestone matching the rest of the building, and in the upper two-thirds a Gothic-style window was made. It is now possible to stand in comfort at the west end of the nave and look out over a wide, unbroken view of Kendal and the surrounding Fells. A new door has been constructed in the south wall. For those who have worshipped there regularly for, say, twenty or thirty years, the advantages of this comparatively new arrangement must be immense.

The interior of the church was rather gloomy, neither was the gloom dispelled by any rich or colourful furnishings. But it was a time of austerity when my attendance there began, and the congregation, small at any time, was further depleted by a number of young men and women joining the Armed Services. I sang in the all-adult choir, and helped with the Sunday School. The old vicar had recently died and he was replaced by a fairly young and extremely fervent man who had been an anthropologist, and then a missionary in Uruguay. I really should not condemn Methodist pulpit thumping, our young vicar positively pounded the pulpit in his ardour – I felt at times that he may well leap, or even fall out, into the congregation to press home his point.

CHAPEL AND CHURCH

There was a single bell operated by a bell rope just inside the west door of the church. Matins began at 10.30am and the system for calling the faithful to worship was thus: at 10.15am the bell was rung for three minutes followed by a two minute break. This was the 'first bell'. At 10.20am the bell was rung again for three minutes followed by a two minute break. This was the 'second bell'. At 10.25am the bell was rung for the third time for three minutes. This was the 'last bell', and if you were still pedalling furiously along Skelsmergh Lane, or pushing your bike up Skelsmergh hill when the last bell was sounding, you knew that you had to jolly well get a move on.

The boy who rang the bell also worked the hand-operated organ blower, and the organist and choirmaster cycled to Skelsmergh from Burneside. He gave me a few elementary organ lessons, and I played for baptisms and once for the wedding of a friend at another church, but I never mastered the pedals sufficiently to make a success of it.

At the age of fourteen I was confirmed, along with eight or nine others, by the Bishop of Carlisle. For girls, white dresses with long sleeves were obligatory. Even my mother conceded that a new white dress was an unnecessary extravagance as it was unlikely ever to be worn again. However, before the War white dresses were the rule on school prize-giving day, so she was able to adapt my sister's 'old' white dress for me to wear on this occasion. A white headscarf, tied under the hair at the back, was also necessary. This caused a minor rumpus when a female visitor at the vicarage, who was helping us to dress, wanted to push my thick, long, curly hair completely out of sight under the headscarf. When I resisted she made a tart remark about, "looking like a Jezebel". I acquiesced until we were out of the vicarage and walking from the lych-gate to the west door, and then I quickly pulled my hair out from under the scarf.

Being confirmed was not a momentous occasion for me. Perhaps it should have been, but I do not recall feeling any different after it was over. However I did have slight feelings of guilt when I went out that evening, escorted by a cadet of the Air Training Corps, to a dance in Kendal. So maybe something touched my conscience after all.

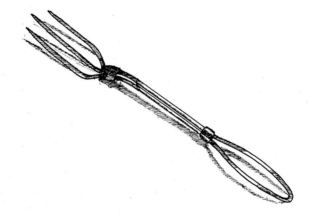

CHAPTER SEVEN

Yorkshire Forbears

My maternal grandparents lived in the West Riding of Yorkshire in the village of Oxenhope. Both were born into large families. My grandfather, Mechi Helliwell, was the fourth of six children born to Sally and Greenwood Helliwell, a farmer of Mouldgreave Farm, Oxenhope, an old Yorkshire long-house. When the sixth child and the only daughter, Julia, was two years old Sally Helliwell died, and my great-grandfather brought up his five sons and little daughter alone.

The given names of three of his sons are worthy of comment. The second son, Milton, was named after the poet, the origins of the name of the third son, Benson, are unknown, and I believe that Mechi, my grandfather, was named after a model farm in Norfolk. Milton remained a bachelor, and Benson emigrated to Australia, married and had two daughters. It was to Melbourne that Julia went to visit her brother and his family, and met the man she eventually married. She returned home to pack her belongings, which included a great quantity of pottery and porcelain, and set out again on the six-week sea voyage to marry Tom Young – a man ten years her junior – in September 1913 when she was thirty-eight years old and he twenty-eight.

They had a house built in Melbourne and she called it "Bronte". But their married happiness was short lived. After only eleven months Tom Young died of pneumonia, and once again, and for the last time, Julia sorrowfully packed her trunks and returned to Haworth to live with her brother Milton. The long and often rough sea voyage took its toll of the crockery and not many pieces survived undamaged.

The Bronte family of Haworth had been very much a part of Greenwood Helliwell's generation. He knew Patrick Bronte as a local vicar, and he attended Charlotte's funeral in the old Haworth Parish Church. It is said that he told of seeing a violet-coloured ribbon hanging out of her coffin.

To a community already steeped in superstition this was yet another ill omen.

My mother as a little girl about the turn of the century remembers the old Mouldgreave being demolished, and oak settles, tables and long case clocks being chopped up for firewood. A new house, retaining the name Mouldgreave, was built on the site, and was no doubt thought of as being greatly superior to the old long-house. And in many ways it would be – less draughty, less damp, less work required to run it and less inconvenient, but certainly less in character and charm.

My grandmother, Emma Procter, was the eldest daughter in a family of nine children born to Elizabeth and James Procter who lived in a hamlet near to Oxenhope called Back-of-Leeming. I believe that they were in fairly poor circumstances compared to my grandfather's family. As a girl, my grandmother had to knit twelve rounds of a sock every evening before she was allowed out of the house to spend time with her friends. With six brothers to knit socks for her task would be never ending, until at the age of twenty-one she married my grandfather, in 1892.

They set up home in Keighley where my mother was born in the following year. My grandfather went into the textile trade and by 1908 had, with his brother-in-law Frank Procter, bought Oxenhope Mill adjacent to the terminus of the Worth Valley Railway. The little family moved house within Oxenhope village a number of times finally settling at Thorn Lea.

Thorn Lea was a semi-detached house, and this one pair of houses stood alone facing the main road entering the village from Cockill Moor; it was not far from the Church, and nearer still to the Methodist Chapel. There was a wooden lattice-work archway over the front gate and the main entrance to the house was at the side. A sitting room at the front, a dining room and kitchen at the back, dark cupboards under the stairs, three bedrooms and a bathroom made it a good, solid stone-built modern house, though it had not yet the benefit of electricity. Gas provided the means of cooking and lighting.

YORKSHIRE FORBEARS

The house was full of furniture, heavy, dark and solid and the best possible that my grand-parents could afford. The dining room held chairs with scratchy horse-hair seats and a chaise longue to match in green-and-black-striped uphol-stery. There was a great mahogany sideboard, its top covered with lacy runners on which stood an imposing glass fruit bowl on a black glass stand and a matching glass biscuit barrel. The sitting room. furniture was more delicate. An Edwardian mahogany suite in Sheraton style, a wooden four-tier cake stand, various side tables, a tea-wagon and a pouffe.

The light shades were made of strings of tiny coloured bugle beads, created by our grandmother herself. The small artefacts which filled most available surfaces were many and varied. I had often heard my grandmother remark, "If I saw anything I liked, I bought it". This was an indication that there was no shortage of money for her to spend on whatever took her fancy. But she was a shrewd and careful housekeeper and manager, and due to the fact that she not only made most of her own clothes, but created all manner of soft furnishings for the house she would have money to spare for the items of brass and copper ware, porcelain and pottery and glassware with which she filled her shelves and cupboards.

CHAPTER EIGHT

Mammam's House

I do not think that my mother ever came to terms with living away from her parents. She was a beloved only child and they had parted with her in marriage very reluctantly. When she was eighteen or nineteen she had been engaged to a young man of twenty-one, John Craven, who had died of tuberculosis. I think that my grandparents felt that she would settle for remaining single, and live with them after this tragedy. And she may well have done so had she not met my father on the Promenade at Morecambe. The courtship in its early stages had to be kept secret from her parents, and all manner of ruses were devised to keep them off the scent. Eventually they became resigned to the marriage and her removal to Westmorland, but visits were made in both directions as often as possible. She returned to Oxenhope whenever she could, taking us with her and leaving my father at home.

My sister and I loved the journey by train and once we had left Kendal behind there were all the familiar things of interest to look out for. Arkholme station with its name picked out in flowers on a background of white stone chippings, Long Preston with its slanting wooden railings and porters marching purposefully up and down the platform calling out, "Long Preston, Long Preston", Wennington where the engine was taken off and more carriages brought up to join ours, and then the engine puffing back again to be coupled up before the exciting journey through the tunnel when the lights in the carriage came on and we had to close the windows. We peered out into the blackness and sometimes saw the shapes of workmen and their lamps. Then there was Hellifield, a busy junction in those days, where a man came along the platform selling chocolate from a tray, and we might have a penny bar of Nestle's milk.

Soon we were in Keighley and quickly across the platform to the Worth Valley train, its little engine puffing and pulling us through Ingrow, Oakworth, Damems, Haworth and finally to Oxenhope. Grandpa was there to meet us and one of the workmen from his mill carried our luggage up the hill to Thorn Lea.

We called our grandmother Mammam, and the first thing we asked for after we had settled in was the dolls' house. This delightful model had been made by Mammam herself. It was about two-and-a-half feet high and one-and-a-half feet wide, and was a house without a front wall. When the pink curtains which covered it were drawn back all the open rooms were revealed. On the ground floor were the kitchen and dining room. Upstairs on the first floor were the bathroom, bedroom and sitting room, and on the top floor, in the loft, was the ballroom. Every room was completely furnished and the ballroom contained a grand piano, a wall mirror decorated with hand-painted flowers, and two dolls in evening gowns and tiaras.

There was also a set of farmyard animals and a zoo. The zoo captured our interest more than the farmyard, which was hardly surprising as at home we were surrounded by farms and farm animals. The zoo was much more exciting. Tall curved pieces of railing could be placed together to keep the zoo animals captive. We had lions, tigers, giraffes, monkeys which we could hang by their tails in the trees, and zebras which we liked best of all. We had not, as yet, been to a real zoo, that would come later and alter our views on wild animals kept in captivity. In the meantime the brightly coloured lead toy animals kept us enthralled.

Tradesmen delivered goods to the house, and those who intrigued me most were the men who sold crumpets from a big shallow tray, and oatcakes which were damp and hung over a pole. Mammam bought several of these and they were transferred from the pole to the wooden clothes-drying rack suspended from the kitchen ceiling where they hung until they were dry and crisp, and were delicious eaten with lumps of butter and sometimes syrup, either for supper or for breakfast.

There were always visits to be made when we stayed at Thorn Lea. First of all we had to go to Keighley, on either bus or train, to see my great-grandmother Granny Procter who lived with her unmarried daughter Aunt Ada and bachelor son Uncle Tom. Aunt Ada was an artist. She painted pictures in oils and embroidered complicated patterns of flowers in silks on tray cloths and tablecloths. Uncle Tom Procter was very dark and rather Spanish looking. He carried lumps of shiny, rock-like licorice in his pockets.

Their house in Redcliffe Street, Keighley, was typically late Victorian and stuffed to bursting point with furniture. There were heavy curtains at the windows and doors, chenille tablecloths which almost reached the floor, all surfaces were covered with ornaments and vases, there were cabinets full of china and glassware, and everywhere a faint smell of gas from the kitchen. In the small flagged yard at the back were the WC and the coal house. I had heard it said that when Spring-cleaning time came round Aunt Ada shovelled the coal out of the coal house, whitewashed the walls, and then shovelled the coal in again. Certainly all was very clean and tidy

There were other brothers, Frank who played the fiddle, Bertie who had a hump on his back and lived in London, and Joe. Frank and Joe were both married, and Joe had been in the First World War. He played the trombone, with a great deal of skill so it was said. It must have been true because tales were told of him playing *The Holy City* as a trombone solo in the Albert Hall, London, in front of King George V and Queen Mary. The musical brothers were known locally as Procter's Band.

There were two other brothers of Mammam's who I never met, and who rejoiced – though that is perhaps not quite the word – in the names of Asa and Pharoah. It was said that when Pharoah married, his wife would not call him by his Christian name (and who could blame her?) instead she called him either "PP" or "Procter".

The things I liked most in Granny Procter's house were the two pot dogs which stood at each end of the very high mantle shelf in the kitchen. They were green and gold with black staring eyes and looked rather fierce. Perhaps fortunately they were well out of reach, as they are today on the top shelf of a plate rack over my dining-room sideboard.

THE GREEN LANES

Granny Procter died when I was about four or five years old and we must have gone to Oxenhope at once because I remember there being a discussion as to which members of the family would sit up all night to watch over the body before the funeral. This was known as the 'Wake', when the living sat all night with the dead to prevent the devil from stealing the soul. Aunt Ada and Uncle Tom continued to live at Redcliffe Street for many years after granny Procter's death.

There were other visits from Thorn Lea. Sometimes we took the bus to Hebden Bridge. The route was over Cockill Moor, through rather inhospitable countryside at any time. It was bleak, even on a sunny day, and in wet weather low cloud and mist swirled over the moors and across the road as the bus toiled up the hill. The bus stopped at a lane-end and we got out and walked up the track to a farmhouse to visit friends of Mammam's for tea. I remember gazing out of the little windows set into the thick stone walls at the wide treeless landscape and wishing the visit would soon come to an end.

Another rather dubious treat was to go to Dorothy and Bertha's. These were two middle-aged spinster sisters who lived at the back of Thorn Lea. Dorothy was a piano teacher and had LRAM after her name, so she was somebody to be in awe of. It must be said that I was not so keen on seeing these ladies as I was to be shown a big doll which was kept in the bottom drawer of a chest. The doll was fully dressed in hand-sewn garments and laid on a little pillow. I longed to touch her, and longed even more to pick her up, but I was never allowed to do either. I could only look at her for a few moments and then the drawer would be closed, and after a few pleasantries had been exchanged between the ladies we would return to Thorn Lea.

Our visits to Oxenhope would not last longer than a week as my father had been left to fend for himself at School House. However much I enjoyed being at my grandparents' house I was always glad and relieved for us to return home to him.

CHAPTER NINE

Removal to School House

When I was nine years old Grandpa Helliwell became ill and had to retire from work at his Mill. It was decided that my grandparents should give up their home and come and live at School House with us. Presumably my mother did much to persuade her parents to make this move and I don't suppose that my father was consulted at all. I find it difficult to understand why Mammam allowed herself to be persuaded. Certainly Grandpa was a sick man, but Mammam was a healthy, capable and very active woman in her early sixties who loved her home, was quite able to nurse her husband, and could well afford help if it was needed.

If, on the other hand, they really wanted to live near to their only daughter, why did they not buy a house in Kendal? Well these questions will never be answered, and so the fact was that they packed up and came to School House

The removal was executed by Ellis Riley, a wiry, dapper, energetic little man who was married to one of Mammam's nieces, and lived at Oakworth. He hired a removal van and drove it himself. Until his illness Grandpa had owned and driven a car which was a Singer touring model with a dicky seat, and which he called "Stella". He and Mammam frequently drove from Oxenhope to Mealbank, which was quite an undertaking in those days. How we loved to be taken for a drive, sitting in the dicky with a travelling rug over our knees, and to eat on the drive a big bar of Motoring chocolate, which we thought was quite the proper thing to do. Presumably Stella was sold when it was realised that Grandpa would not drive again, and he and Mammam arrived at School House in the removal van.

It was a fine day and I skipped about in the front garden watching chairs and tables and boxes full of china being carried from the van either into the house or to be stored in the cellar. Some items eventually had to be disposed of, and a yellow porcelain tea-set with black handles and an opalescent finish was sold to Aunties for five shillings.

We were somewhat in awe of the grandfather clock. It had come from Granny Procter, and tradition decreed that it must pass to the eldest daughter of the family otherwise there would be a tragedy. So it became Mammam's and then my mother's. However, somewhere along the line before it came to Mammam it was taken out of the family and the unfortunate recipient of it drowned herself in Leeshaw reservoir. I think it is extremely unlikely that this suicide had anything to do with the clock, but Mammam was a very superstitious woman and she saw the drowning as a portent. So the clock was looked upon as something we were stuck with whether we liked it or not, and we didn't like it much for it had a loud and unlovely strike.

Young children accept altered situations fairly readily and we settled down quickly to School House being full of people and furniture. Mammam and Grandpa occupied the back bedroom and the front sitting room, but it wasn't long before Grandpa's health deteriorated and he was no longer able to shuffle about. He took to his bed, which by now had become the bed-settee in the sitting-room to make it easier for those who were looking after him.

The day before he died Mammam fell downstairs and broke her leg and was taken off to hospital and kept there. Imagine my mother's distress. We were not very happy either at the thought of our dead Grandpa lying in his coffin in the front sitting-room, and when we had to pass the door on our way up and down stairs we ran as fast as we could. So my father said to my mother, "I think they should see him and then they won't be so frightened". He took us both by the hand and led us into the sitting-room. We stood for a moment looking at Grandpa's face above the silken shroud. It was pale, smooth and peaceful, and that seemed to calm our fears.

REMOVAL TO SCHOOL HOUSE

The funeral was a big affair. Many people came from the West Riding and there were masses of elaborate wreaths and floral crosses. "Bury him with ham", being a Yorkshire custom, was strictly adhered to and we all sat down to a sumptuous meal at the Fleece Inn, Kendal.

Mammam was never quite the same after her husband's death. She now occupied the bed settee on her return from hospital and we ran to and fro with drinks, Marmite sandwiches in Turog brown bread, and digestive biscuits. When Doctor Craig came to remove the plaster from her leg I was allowed to watch and I was terrified that he would cut Mammam's flesh with the big, sharp shears.

Learning to walk again was a long and slow process, but when she could at last walk up and down the stairs the sitting-room returned to normal and she lived with us as one of the family

I suppose it worked quite well. Undoubtedly Mammam was a great help in the house, in the kitchen and with the sewing, and when my mother returned from shopping expeditions the tea would be ready. And we soon discovered that Mammam could provide almost anything we needed. Pieces of material for doll's clothes, pens, paper, cards, items of jewellery, belts, purses, scarves, clothes for dressing up, and if she hadn't got it she would make it. Nothing, it seemed, was beyond her. For example she made bags of all shapes and sizes from all manner of materials; there was everything from beaded evening purses to shopping bags. In those days milk bottles had cardboard tops which fitted just inside the bottle. A tiny disc in the centre could be pressed in with the finger to lift the cardboard top out. Mammam saved all the bottle tops, washed and dried them, covered them with brightly coloured wool (which probably came from a jumper which she had unravelled), stitched them together, put in a lining and handles, and there was a new and unusual shopping bag.

There was a craze in the 1930s for making 'Stamen' jewellery, and my mother and Mammam fell for this in a big way. One bought a kit which consisted of the metal base, including the pin and the clips, of brooches and earrings, tubes of putty-coloured cement to spread on the base, and the stamens which of course were like the stamens of a flower and were very short pins with a bulbous head. They were available in many colours and finishes, and were stuck into the cement in any design and colour one chose. School House became a small factory while the craze lasted. Relatives and friends received them as presents, and we even sold some. It must be said that the finished products were most artistically designed and very attractive.

My father called Mammam's bedroom, "The Upper Museum". It was packed from floor to ceiling with boxes, and more boxes filled all the space under the bed. Mammam was a poor sleeper and it was not unusual for her to spend much of the night sitting up in bed trimming hats or crocheting collars or scarves. She was meticulous in her dress and everything had to match. She had outfits galore, and matching hat, shoes and bag for each one. She only went out once a week, to Kendal on a Saturday morning, so her smart clothes did not see daylight very often. And while they were hanging in the wardrobe and folded in the drawers they were preserved in mothballs, the smell of which never really disappeared.

Some of the dressing-table drawers were full of boxes of jewellery and fashion accessories. I loved to look at the necklaces and try them on. "These are real amber", or, "these are called 'Job's Tears'", Mammam would say. There were jet brooches, fashionable during Queen Victoria's long years of mourning – one had a lock of hair in it; and lovely pale cameos, "this belonged to your great-great Aunt Emma". There were rings and earrings but these latter were all for pierced ears. Mammam's ears had been pierced, but now as an elderly lady the holes in the ear lobes could be clearly seen and the lobes drooped from the the weight of the rings. I believe I decided then and there that I would never have my ears pierced.

It was my job to take her a cup of tea in the morning because Mammam did not get up early. Invariably I was asked to hand her the small flask of brandy from the cylindrical, marble-topped mahogany bedside cabinet. I held the cup and saucer while Mammam poured what she called a teaspoonful of brandy into the tea. The brandy was always allowed to run over the spoon by two or three times the amount. Sometimes she would have a cigarette – she smoked a brand called 'Piccadilly' which were small and bought in a dark blue oval tin, and she used an amber cigarette holder. In the middle of the morning her tipple was a raw egg, beaten in a glass of milk often with sherry added

When she died at the age of eighty-two there was the most remarkable sorting out of her personal belongings. We counted over one hundred pairs of shoes and an equal number of handbags stored under her bed.

And what were we to do with it all? By this time I was married and had a baby son and was living ninety miles away, so I had very little to do with the upheaval. All the shoes were too large for my mother, sister, Aunts and myself. Many were nearly new. So my mother sent dozens of pairs to the Mill for the mill-girls to share out among themselves, and handbags no doubt found their way to relatives and friends. A bonfire was built outside the back garden of School House, and thus the less desirable items of clothing were consumed.

CHAPTER TEN

Shopping and Village Characters

There was no village shop as such in Mealbank but during my early childhood several enterprising women sold provisions and home-produced food from their cottage doors. Home-made toffee was sold by Mrs Grisedale at Gatehouse Cottages near Hayfell bridge.

It was a steep climb up the big hill from Aunties' house to Hayfell bridge, and in Auntie Sally's company the pace was very slow indeed. Not that we minded or ever thought of hurrying; there was so much to see on the way. We knew every bumpy rock and every stone on the rough and uneven road. In wet weather rain water ran down the hill in rivulets washing away the fine loose earth and pebbles, leaving the bigger stones and rocks so prominent that it was hardly a suitable surface for any wheeled vehicles. We were familiar with the bright green mosses and the tiny ferns which grew amongst the grey, lichen-covered stones of the wall. We knew just where to look in the grassy bank for wild violets, and in the bushes for birds' nests. In the autumn we gathered hazel nuts and rose hips, and sometimes berried holly.

The railway emerged from the cutting at Hayfell bridge on its long climb from Oxenholme up to Shap, and ran past Rock Cottages on the village side of the bridge and Gatehouse Cottages on the other side of the bridge, which took the Appleby road over it.

Mrs Grisedale at Gatehouse Cottages made two kinds of toffee, Everton and treacle, and we bought a pennyworth of whichever we fancied most. The main fascination of this expedition was not the purchasing and receiving of the toffee but the deft way a square of thick, putty-coloured paper was magically twisted and formed into a perfect cone-shaped bag to hold the irregularly shaped toffee pieces.

At the aforementioned Rock Cottages, just above the little reservoir where the railway line bisected her front garden,

Mrs Florey Hutton emerged as a provider of some necessities. She baked brown bread and sold cigarettes and pop, vegetables and flowers from her garden, and eggs from her hens. At Christmas time she took orders for wreaths and crosses which she made from interwoven branches of holly, yew and fir, gathered from the hedges round about.

Mrs Hutton's water supply came from a spring on the hill Benson Knott; it flowed under the railway and she drew it by means of a hand-operated pump in her front garden. Though plentiful, water was not so easy to obtain and was cold into the bargain. Nothing unusual in that of course; School House was one of only three houses in the village to have a hot water supply. Mrs H. was, however, not one to waste it. Her water was heated in an iron kettle over the fire, as it was in most houses, and she washed up in a big enamel bowl on the kitchen table, there being no sink. Whenever I called, which was quite often if my mother had run out of cigarettes or brown bread, this big washing-up bowl was full of very dirty water, and Mrs Hutton was washing out pots and pans and baking tins, and I did wonder if they came out cleaner than when they went in.

She was a very dark person. Her hair was jet-black, her eyes like two black hat-pins and her skin dark and swarthy like a gipsy's. Though always pleasant and kind she was nevertheless a very shrewd business woman. Very early on Saturday mornings this good lady could be observed wheeling her ancient bicycle on the road to Kendal, the machine weighed down on handlebars, seat and carrier with her home-made and home-grown produce to sell in Kendal market. After a good day's business she was able to ride the bicycle on the return journey home.

As well as from Mrs Hutton eggs could be bought from one of the cottages half-way down the hill from School House to the Mill, and sometimes I was sent down the hill to buy half-a-dozen. On one of these occasions, as my mother handed me the money to pay for the eggs, she said, "Ask Mrs Dobson how her leg is". Mrs Dobson was a very slim, dark-haired woman, perhaps about thirty-eight or forty, scrupulously clean and always attired in a long flowered apron. As she put the eggs into my basket I said, "And Mammy says, how is your leg?". She leaned towards me and in a conspiratorial whisper in my ear said, "Tell her, I wish they'd cut the bugger off!"

I don't think that this startling remark had much effect on me other than to make me wonder why anyone should actually want to have their leg cut off. I returned home with the eggs and repeated the conversation to my parents. Their reactions were entirely predictable. My father's shoulders shook with silent laughter, and my mother's outrage soon gave way to reluctant amusement.

To complete the list of unofficial shop-keepers, in the middle of the village Mrs Morphet sold groceries, sweets, tobacco and cigarettes, and Alexander's Pure Table Waters from her front sitting-room. Pure Table Waters they may have been, but to us it was all Pop, whether it was Dandelion and Burdock, Vimto or Lemonade. The first remembered bottles were thick, unclear glass, sealed with a glass alley, or marble, which to our small hands and fingers took some knocking down to open the bottle, even with the correct wooden implement.

All these little establishments were handy if you ran short of, say, a bag of sugar or flour on baking day, or if you were unexpectedly given a penny to buy sweets, but the main grocery supplies were bought in the town and could be delivered, free of charge, to those who did not want to or were not able to carry them home.

In our case a traveller from one of the high-class grocers called at the house every Monday morning, and the goods were delivered on the Thursday. Mr Welch came in his Morris 8, waddled down the garden path up the steps to the back door and sat down heavily and rather out of breath at the dining-table. He opened his tiny attaché case and took out his order book with two carbon papers. I sat down at the other side of the table and wrote down the order in my own exercise book.

Mr Welch was a short, dark, thickset man with a black moustache. He interested me because I had heard my mother say that his wife had been in the Asylum for many years and would remain there until she died. So Mr Welch was a man to treat with sympathy and respect.

My mother's grocery order varied little from week to week, except of course at Christmas, and as her only means of cooking was a paraffin stove and oven this fuel was always the first item on the order. It was written down by Mr Welch in what I thought was a most curious manner, thus: ✗ paraffin; and during a lull in the ordering, while my mother thought about what she would order next, he reinforced the dots in the symbol with the pencil over and over again until it looked like a hot cross bun. From that day to this I have never known the meaning of the 'X' and the dots.

Aunties bought their groceries from the Co-op in the town, and these were delivered in a big, grey truck, the cartons of provisions being covered only by a green and flapping tarpaulin.

The Co-op grocery was a wide and drab corner shop with a bare wooden floor and a perpetual odour of stale cheese. It was devoid of colourful displays and seemed to be staffed entirely by greasy-haired men in grubby white coats who rarely spoke or smiled. There was, however, one attraction in this rather seedy establishment and that was the method of payment for goods. In one corner of the shop sat a young woman inside a little office with windows all round it. From a point above this office thick wires radiated to various places over the counters. On these wires, and on two wheels, ran little cylindrical containers. The bottom half of the container, made of wood and polished by constant handling, was unscrewed by the assistant; the money and the chit with the amount spent was put into it, the container was screwed up, a handle pulled, and the container made to whizz along the wires to the office with the windows where the girl took out the money, sorted the change and sent it whizzing back along the wire to the counter.

Our high-class grocers was something of a contrast. A bright, smart, colourful shop, full of appetising sides of bacon and ham, fresh and interestingly-shaped cheeses, attractive displays of pickles and preserves, polished wooden display stands filled with bars of chocolate (Terry's *Oliver*

Twist and Rowntree's *Plain York* were favourites), and tins of an endless variety of biscuits, covered by lift-up glass lids and sold loose in any quantity required. Deciding which biscuits to buy required concentration, especially when so many were delicious. Should I choose Gypsy Creams, thick, round, chocolate-and-coconut-flavoured shortcakes sandwiched together with chocolate cream? Or perhaps chocolate Viennas, triangular wafers covered with dark chocolate? Or my great favourites, Playtime, semi-sweet biscuits covered with coloured icing and a picture on each biscuit picked out in contrasting icing sugar, each picture depicting a game being played? Among my mother's favourites were Café Noir, which were covered in coffee-flavoured icing. My father's tastes were much plainer. He was fond of ginger nuts, which he dipped in his tea before eating. Aunties baked their own biscuits, Shrewsbury and ginger snaps, but sometimes bought Marie and Osborne which we thought very plain and dull, though one plain biscuit which I really enjoyed was called Thick Tea. They were an inch thick, and spread liberally with butter soon filled up a corner when I was feeling hungry. Thick Tea biscuits were bought at Mrs Bateman's, a tiny shop in Stramongate which was approached down three or four little steps and presided over by Miss Bateman, a large, blonde lady who exuded efficiency and authority together with the right amount of friendliness and charm. This little shop specialised in what we thought of as luxury foods, honey, rum butter, rich and sickly chocolate cakes, home-made toffee and my mother's favourite fudge, which came in many flavours.

Small wonder that my mother's extravagant tastes ran riot, and in our high-class grocer's with its all-pervading air of freshly ground coffee and smoked bacon, she ran up another big order in addition to the weekly one. The goods were brought in a large cardboard carton to the bus-stop near the railway station by a boy on a delivery bicycle, and the services of one or two of the village boys were secured to carry the carton up the hill from the Mill to School House, and a small payment made for their efforts.

THE GREEN LANES

The weekly shopping trips to Kendal and the frequent purchases from the various village ladies were necessary mainly because there were no means of keeping and storing perishable items of food at home. There were no freezers and no refrigerators. Houses which had a pantry, like Aunties', probably had a cold slab on which could be stood the milk and butter, but food such as fresh fish, bacon, sausages, meat pies and fresh meat could only be kept for a day or two before being cooked, especially in warm weather, so these commodities had to be bought in small quantities and bought often.

I have only dealt here with going out to shop. There were some alternatives available.

CHAPTER ELEVEN

Visiting Salesmen

In addition to the items which could be bought in the village, and the shopping expeditions to Kendal, several travelling salesmen called during the week. The most vital and necessary of these was the coalman. Every house in the village bought coal, and together with wood and sticks it was the main means of heating and in most cases of cooking too. Almost everyone cooked over the open fire and baked in the fireside oven. Hot water was only obtained by heating it in a pan or kettle on the fire, so fuel was of the utmost importance.

One or two houses including our own had a small portable electric fire which could be used in any room in an emergency, but this was seldom necessary. We had never experienced a heated bedroom – even though each one had a tiny fireplace – and in the very cold weather we just accepted the fact that the rooms would be icy, and we nipped smartly into bed with our hot water bottles.

The Co-op were the sole providers of coal. Doubtless there were other solid fuel merchants, but here at any rate the Co-op had the monopoly. I don't think that I ever knew the coalman's name, but he was a kindly and pleasant fellow, big-framed and broad-shouldered as indeed he needed to be, and rather stooping which wasn't surprising. It was a continual source of amazement to me, as a five- or six-year-old, how he could carry sack after sack of coal and heave it over his shoulder into the waiting empty coal house, day after day, week after week and year after year, because this same man delivered our coal for years. I would tramp round the top row of cottages with him on his delivery rounds almost mesmerised by the thick grime on his face and hands, and once I even dared to ask him, in all innocence, if he ever got washed.

Coal was always delivered on Monday. I felt that this was a very awkward day to bring it, as on fine Mondays all the washing was hanging out and the coalman either had to dodge under the lines of clothes, which was anything but easy with a ten-stone bag of coal on his back, or each house-wife had to rush out and unpeg the garments which were hanging in his path.

One bag of coal cost five shillings and that was all that most households could afford. My mother bought two bags as we often had two fires in winter, one in the dining-room and one in the front sitting-room. At ten shillings for two bags my father called it black diamonds, so sticks were gathered to supplement the coal supply and also initially to light the fire.

Our sticking expeditions into the woods took place per-haps once a week. Much depended on the weather. If it was fine and dry and if I was on holiday from school we went during the day; sometimes during the summer we would go in the evening. My parents and sister never went sticking but Aunties were almost always involved, – their lives were more leisurely and their days at home saw little activity. Dressed in their hats and long cardigans and aprons they accompanied me wearing my oldest clothes and shoes. I pushed the big shabby dolls' pram, now bereft of hood and apron and dolls, with Glen our Cairn terrier waddling along at the side and Chintz the marmalade cat stepping daintily along several yards behind, tail in the air.

Most of my childhood leisure time was spent in the woods. I knew them intimately in all seasons, in every kind of weather, and at all times of day. They sheltered my body from sun, wind and rain and they were a certain solace for my spirit whatever my mood. If I was happy then the woods were joyous, sometimes full of new growth and bird-song, or of falling leaves and the splittering sound of them trodden underfoot among twigs and the mossy roots of old trees, or of boughs laden with dazzling snow and birds looking for food. If I was sad then the woods were sombre too, quiet yet peaceful, with only the distant chirrups of birds; and if I wanted solitude and tranquility then there I surely found it. But whatever the season and whatever the mood, going into the woods was always an adventure.

VISITING SALESMEN

On our sticking expeditions the woods were alive with noise and crackle. Auntie Sally, who was not strong enough to gather sticks, took her little camp stool and sat and watched us at work. First we filled the bottom of the pram with kindling – thin, dry, brittle sticks broken into small pieces to light the fire. Then came sticks of the next size. Sometimes we picked them up from the ground where they had fallen, sometimes we broke them off the trees. We soon learned to tell which wood was dead and which was green. When we had filled the pram we looked around for really big sticks which were too strong to break, and these we trailed behind us. Thus the procession made its way back home. First the pram piled high with sticks, and Glen – who was too old and fat and out of breath to walk – lying on top of the sticks, panting. I pushed the pram followed by one or two cronies who had joined us trailing sticks behind them. Next Auntie Mary with a vast bundle of sticks in her arms, and last of all Auntie Sally, almost tip-toeing along, carrying her camp stool, with Chintz the cat by her side.

And so it was that my father always had a good stock of kindling and was able to saw up the bigger sticks into logs which were kept to stoke the fire on winter evenings. Once the business of keeping the fires burning had been resolved attention could be turned to food and other goods and services offered for sale at the door.

Fresh fish, probably from the Fleetwood area, was brought to the village once a week by a man driving a three-wheeled motor tricycle van. My mother was a good customer. She always bought either plaice, hake or halibut, and I would stand at the open back doors of the little van and watch the fishman fillet the plaice on a thick wooden board, well worn and covered with deep knife cuts. The man would lay one of his red hands, scattered about with fish scales, flat on the fish while he filleted it with his sharp knife: two fillets with white skin and two with fawn skin and orange spots. Hake and halibut were not filleted but cut into thick steaks. The fish was carried in the weighing scale pan to the back door where my mother had a big plate ready to receive it.

THE GREEN LANES

On two evenings a week Greenwood's the bakers from Kendal brought bread, teacakes, cakes and pastries. As my mother did all her own baking it wasn't very often that we patronised this firm but we did sometimes spend some of our pocket monet, a penny or maybe even twopence, on the sort of cakes which were not baked at home: a chocolate eclair, a cream horn or a vanilla slice.

In summer the Italian ice-cream vendors visited us on several evenings a week in their gaily painted vans. No chiming tunes to announce their arrival, but a blast on the Claxon horn. Far and away the best value for money was a pennyworth in a cup, and the amount spooned into the cup varied according to whether it was Joseph's or Tognarelli's van visiting, and indeed on who was the driver and salesman. A halfpenny cornet was bought for the dog, and on the rare occasions when the van was very late I was allowed to eat a small cornet sitting up in bed.

There were a number of itinerant callers during the year, men who wanted to clean the drains and a man on a bicycle with a grindstone who would sharpen knives, scissors and shears. There was no custom for them at School House as drain problems were attended to by men from the Mill and my father sharpened all the tools with his own carborundum stone.

Then there were the tramps. The tramps travelled alone and called at the back door, holding up an enamel billy-can and asking my mother to make them some tea, which she always did, at the same time cutting two big slices of jam and bread which she wrapped in a parcel. I was often sent to hand over the billy-can of tea and the jam sandwiches, and twopence, to the gentleman of the road who sat respectfully outside the gate. It was always received most appreciatively, until the day I followed one tramp who I instinctively felt was up to no good and saw him pitch the parcel of food into the hedge bottom and utter an oath. No doubt he would rather have had money for beer. I ran back to tell my mother what I had seen. I think she was a little wary of feeding tramps after that.

VISITING SALESMEN

One of my mother's favourite door-to-door salesmen was the Breton onion man. He carried the strings of onions on a bicycle. Just where he and his outfit had set forth from was a mystery. I think my mother fell a little in love with his dark good looks, his intriguing accent and his outrageous charm. It was not difficult for him to talk her into buying two long strings of onions each time he called. The onions hung behind the back door, together with the leather strap – used for corporal punishment – and my father's working coat and cap.

Occasionally one man, or two men together, would call with a roll of carpet or linoleum on their shoulders. They must have carried it from Kendal unless they had a truck parked somewhere outside the village. They wore suits and trilby hats and in the summer looked very sweaty. It must have been devastating to have carried a roll of linoleum for possibly two-and-a-half miles, hawked it around the village, not sold it, and have to carry it back again. But in fact I believe they quite often made a sale. They would sell their goods considerably cheaper than the man who brought it on a horse and cart, and to buy it from a shop in the town would cost very much more.

From all I have described by way of local shops and visiting salesmen it would appear that the village was well catered for both inwardly and outwardly. Tastes were simple and varied little; choice was limited and pockets were not well lined, but everyone had enough to eat, a fire in the grate, and as well as everyday attire they had a hat and coat for Sunday Best.

CHAPTER TWELVE

Wheels

Whether or not we were aware of it wheels played a very important part in our young lives. Only two families in the village owned a car, and we were not one of them.

Nearby farmers did not frequent the village but were to be seen riding the lanes around their land on very dirty, creaking bicycles or sitting at the front of a loaded, horse-drawn cart in the course of their daily labours. Saturday morning saw them trotting in style in a pony and trap to market and to the shops in Kendal, wearing their best suits and with their wives sitting bolt upright by their side. The trap would be packed with baskets of eggs, butter, jars of jam and a few chickens plucked and ready for the oven, all to sell at a market stall.

There were buses, but a normal-sized single-decker bus of the type run by the bus companies would not have been able to negotiate the steep hills and sharp corners on the unmade roads leading into and out of the centre of the village. Two buses brought workers to the Mill early in the morning and took them home again at half-past five, but this was a privately run service and did not carry other passengers.

A bus service ran between Kendal and Appleby three or four times a day, the picking up points for villagers being Hayfell Bridge or Scalthwaiterigg Stocks which necessitated a walk of half to three-quarters of a mile. It was quite a common occurrence for the bus to be full when it arrived at either of these points and to fly past leaving intending passengers completely stranded. The only course of action then was either to abandon the trip and return home or to walk the two-and-a-half miles to the town.

To take shoppers from the village into Kendal a private taxi firm, Mitchell's, ran what would now be called a mini-bus.

THE GREEN LANES

This bus came into the centre of the village and turned round in the clearing around the ash tree. Down to town at two-o'clock and back at six on three days a week and three times on Saturday. This service was not completely reliable however, and if the bus was wanted elsewhere or had broken down (which quite often happened) then one or two taxis were sent. If there was only one taxi, and eight or ten people were waiting, it had to make two journeys. And so this kind of bus travel in these particular circumstances was more of an endurance test than a pleasure.

In any event there was never enough room in the cars even though they were high, wide and opulent. The upholstery was thick, deep velvet and the chromium plating lavish and gleaming. Three people could sit comfortably on the back seat, but having flopped down had to fight their way up again when it was time to disembark. Two small seats could be unfolded in front of the back seat. A plate glass partition divided the driver and front seat passenger from those in the back. There were moveable arm rests, ash-trays which opened and closed, and tasselled strap hangers which performed more or less the same functions as present day seat belts though in a rather different manner. However none of these luxuries compensated for the overall inconvenience caused to passengers by this substitute for the bus.

Even though I was six years old when I started school a full day's schooling was thought by my mother to be too much for me, though I was far from being delicate. Consequently I had school dinner and returned home on an early afternoon bus on the Appleby route, and I hated it. The bus was always crowded, and on at least two days a week full of noisy farmers returning home from the Auction Mart. There was also Mrs Turner.

Mrs Turner lived alone in a wooden caravan in a field just off Paddy Lane. She was, I suppose, a gipsy, but we did not think of her as such. She was not like the groups of gipsies who were familiar sights in the area from time to time. Village boys called her a witch and we were rather afraid of her. I dreaded her coming to sit next to me on the bus. It must be said that she was very dirty and her breath smelled strongly of beer. Her face was cadaverous and she had no teeth and her nostrils were brown with constant snuff-taking. She wore an old felt hat and a long, tightly-fitting coat with a bedraggled fur collar, and she carried two big shopping bags filled to capacity with what looked like rags. If all the front seats were taken – and I had to sit at the back – I was terrified that the conductor would not reach me to take my fare before the bus arrived at the Stocks. I sat there, every muscle taut, my heart pounding, until I could say, "The Stocks". Even then I had little confidence that the bus would stop. Suppose the conductor forgot to press the buzzer and the bus flew past the Stocks? I could of course alight at Hayfell bridge which was the next stop, but that cost another penny which I did not have, and more importantly I was met at the Stocks. But the bus always did stop at the Stocks and the relief which swept over me was too great to be imagined. And there, resting on her camp stool, waiting for me, was dear little Auntie Sally.

Village children did not have scooters. The wheels would not stand up to the rough roads. One or two were tried but very soon fell apart. The three-wheeled 'Fairy Cycle' did not have the staying power either. So the village boys concocted four-wheels-and-a-board from odd pieces of wood left lying around and wheels from abandoned perambulators. These vehicles were strictly male, far too dangerous and undignified for any girl to attempt to drive one.

At about six years of age on to the scene of pedal power came my high-class Triang Tricycle. Brand new, this was vastly superior to anything owned by my contemporaries. I tore around on it for several years, often carrying a passenger standing on the back; had the manufacturers only known, it must have been the best possible advertisement for their product. Eventually of course I graduated to a full-size bicycle. Zelia had for some time owned a 'racer', a bicycle with drop-handlebars. This one bought second-hand was painted silver and we thought it was the ultimate in bicycles. She was never the keen cyclist that I was and it wasn't long before she abandoned bicycle for bus.

THE GREEN LANES

My first real bicycle was bought from my cousin Laura when I was twelve years old. It was a Hercules and I christened it Horace. A year or two later – when I was struggling with geometry theorems – the name Pythagoras was added and it was always referred to by everyone as. Horace Pythagoras. I lived on it; and perfected the art of cycling without hands all the way from Laverock Bridge to the first houses at the entrance to the town. In fact I kept Horace until long after I was married, and only at the age of twenty seven – a year after the birth of my son – did I acquire for the first time in my life a brand new bicycle.

CHAPTER THIRTEEN

More Village Characters

One or two village women were willing to be hired out to do rough or heavy work for those who were not capable or not strong enough to undertake it for themselves.

One of these able bodies came to help with our washing. She was called, aptly enough, Mrs White. She was a big, bony woman, broad in the beam, bad on her feet and with a lugubrious countenance. Her ample torso was swathed in a stiff white apron, and she rarely smiled which was perhaps not surprising as she had six children to look after and her husband was said to be rather too keen on the bottle and not keen enough on work.

Wash day really meant the whole day being devoted to it. My father would get up at six-thirty and light the fire under the sett pot in the cellar. This was a receptacle for the boiling of the white clothes and its capacity was three or four times that of a tub in a modern washing machine. The sett pot or 'copper' – because it was often made of copper – was shaped like an eggshell cut across in half, and it was built into a square of bricks in one corner of the cellar, with a fire in a cavity in the bricks underneath and a flue going up the wall and out into the open.

There was an old brown stone sink with a single cold tap in the cellar and water from this tap was carried in a lading can (a large cylindrical tin can with a handle, holding about half a gallon) to fill the copper, and with the fire roaring underneath the water soon heated up.

Many items could be washed at the kitchen sink – as we had hot water in the house from a fireback boiler – but big items, – sheets, bedspreads, curtains and overalls were put into a zinc 'peggy tub' (like a dustbin but wider) and bashed about with either a posser, a deep upside-down copper saucer full of holes and fastened to a wooden shaft, or swirled about with the doll legs, a circular piece of wood with four wooden legs all fixed to a wooden shaft.

When all the clothes had been washed and some boiled, and then rinsed (a back-breaking job this), they had to be mangled. The mangle was a massive, free-standing, cast-iron affair with large wooden rollers. Very effective for squeezing out the water but they also broke any buttons, curtain hooks and rings if you had unfortunately forgotten to remove them first. One of my jobs if I was at home was to twine, that is to turn the handle of, the mangle. I did this with enormous gusto. As she guided the clothes through the rollers Mrs White looked more disapproving and more funereal than ever.

There was a separate wash-house for the cottages in Woodside Terrace where Aunties lived. This was a little stone building across the path from their back gates. It housed the wash-tubs and the mangles, the handles of which were chained and padlocked to the legs of the machine when not in use so that they could not be tampered with.

On a fine windy day the lines of clothes soon blew dry, but on damp and rainy days the wet, limp garments had to be draped and hung over clothes horses and set around the fire. What a misery it was in the winter not to be able to see the fire let alone get near to it, and the nasty, steamy smell pervading the room.

When the washing was finished the copper and the peggy tub had to be emptied by means of the lading-can into a grate in the middle of the flagged floor of the cellar, all receptacles cleaned out, the rollers of the mangle dried and a clean cloth put between them, the fire under the copper raked out and the floor mopped and dried. No wonder it took almost all day. There was no time for a cooked midday meal, it was always cold meat from the Sunday joint (with bread and butter), because wash-day was Monday, rain, hail or snow, and that was an end to it; no other day would do. Tea might be more ambitious but after the rigours of the day, even with the strong arm of Mrs White to help, my mother was rarely equal to the task of producing a big meal.

The ironing was tackled the next day. Blankets were spread over one end of the dining table and covered with an old flannelette sheet, brown with many scorch marks. Here my mother ironed the clothes with an electric iron which had to be continually switched off and on as there was no fabric guide and no thermostat. I was allowed to iron the handkerchiefs but found the iron very heavy indeed.

Auntie Mary ironed on the floor. She spread old blankets and a sheet on the carpet and knelt down to the task. She had no electric iron. A flat iron was heated at the fire and tested for heat either on a piece of newspaper or on the edge of the sheet. The flat iron might stay hot long enough to iron one or two small garments before it needed to be heated up again on the bar in front of the fire. Ironing in Aunties' house might occupy the whole morning or the whole afternoon but at least Auntie Mary – for it was always she who did the ironing – could sit and take a rest while the iron was heating up.

What a chore it was, even when all was dry and ironed, to have to sew the buttons onto the garments again. It could take a whole evening, and if curtains had been washed all the brass rings and hooks had to be sewn on again as well. Of all modern kitchen inventions I am sure that the washing machine is the greatest.

Another able-bodied, broad-beamed woman was Mrs Dickinson. She it was who obliged with hanging paper on the walls and white-washing the ceilings, and Aunties were among her regular customers. Mrs D. lived in the middle of the village and on the day appointed for the decorating at Woodside Terrace she was to be seen marching steadily up the hill attired in a long and voluminous black skirt, a jumper bared to the bosom, black stockings and a sacking apron, her cheeks red and weather-beaten, her thin hair scraped back from her face into a bun, and one tooth in her mouth and that in the centre of her lower jaw. Definitely a woman of no nonsense and few utterances but those few much to the point and delivered in sharp and rasping tones.

Her husband was always referred to as John Tom, except by my father who called him Jack. He was a small man and generally thought to be henpecked. He worked under my father at the Mill, and whether he was a bit lacking in the top garrett or really a bit of a dry wit I was never sure, but my father used to entertain us with tales of what John Tom had said on certain occasions. One of these tales, which as children we never tired of hearing, went thus:

John Tom appeared at work one day with his left hand heavily bandaged. "What's the matter with your hand, Jack?" asked my father. "Well Teddy, it was like this", said John Tom, "I was chopping wood, and the axe slipped and I nearly took my thumb off". "Oh dear, I'm sorry", said my father, "take care, and look after it". "Oh I will, Teddy, thank ye, but God knaws what would 'ave 'appened if I'd 'ad 'od of t'axe wi' beath 'ands".

John Tom was one of the characters of the village. Another was Arthur Bell, although not strictly a villager as he lived about a mile-and-a-half distant. He was one of the signalmen at Hayfell Bridge signal box and as such worked shifts. He could be observed going on duty marching at the double all the way up the steep hill from the Mill to the railway line – about a mile – a small, thin, wiry man in railway uniform, his lunch basket slung by a piece of string round his back and wearing enormous hob-nailed boots which gave him the appearance of Mickey Mouse. He kept up this remarkable pace long after he was sixty and when stopped by someone enquiring after his health he would shout, "Niver better. Niver better".

The sight of an elderly Roman Catholic priest on the fringe of a village so predominantly Methodist was to say the least incongruous. Father Fleming lived at Dodding Green, a house of great antiquity standing in a triangle of land between Laverock bridge, Skelsmergh and Scarfoot. It was built towards the end of the 14th century by William Dodding, and at the end of the 17th century was repaired and restored by a new owner, Robert Stephenson, who wished to make it a place for prayer and worship and a permanent home for a Roman Catholic priest. It was not until the end of the 18th century that the little chapel in the house was registered and licensed for free public worship.

Apart from the occupants of the Lodge at the entrance to Dodding Green there was in the 1930s only one Roman

Catholic family in Mealbank, and as the only child of that family was my best friend in the village I knew Father Fleming a little better than most village children did. We were rather afraid of him in the same way that we were afraid of nuns and anyone who was completely dressed in black, and of ghosts, who were in our lively imagination always swathed in white.

It was generally understood that Father Fleming's health was not good. He stooped badly, was unsteady on his feet and always used a walking cane with an amber handle. His hands had rather a horrid fascination because the flesh was purple, except where it was stained deep yellow with nicotine, and his nails were long and claw-like. His teeth too were long and very yellow. This poor, kind man would not have hurt a fly. His whole manner was gentle and soft and he loved children, to whom he was forever dispensing sweets from the pockets of his black overcoat. He often travelled to Kendal on Mitchell's bus, especially on Saturday afternoons when it was known that he frequented the cinema, and of course as I have already indicated he was a very heavy smoker.

Muriel – the daughter of the Roman Catholic family – and I walked to Dodding Green along Skelsmergh Lane from Laverock bridge. The swiftly flowing river on the left is somewhat deeper and steadier here as it emerges from under the bridge. Oak, rowan, hazel and holly trees grow along its banks, their trunks leaning towards those growing on the opposite bank, their roots partially submerged in the water. The right-hand side of the lane is bounded by a dry-stone wall covered in mosses and ivy, and in the grass at the base of it are speedwell, birds'-foot trefoil and clover.

Dodding Green Lodge stood at the gateway to the House. Here lived the Fagans, an Irish family of three, – mother, father and daughter Marcella who was a friend of Zelia's. Mr Fagan was a road-mender and spent much of his time keeping Skelsmergh Lane tidy and in good order. His face resembled a withered russet apple, and no wonder for he was out in all weathers in fustian breeches with lumps of sacking tied over the knees, and when it rained a sack fastened around his shoulders. After the Fagans left the lodge it was again occupied until after the War but was then demolished leaving no trace.

Muriel and I walked through the big gates and along the drive to the front of the House which is almost hidden by trees. The door was opened by the housekeeper and we were invited inside where Father Fleming showed us around the house and the chapel and pointed out to us the priests' hiding places. I was aware even then what a beautiful house it was with its long, low-ceilinged rooms, lovely woodwork and outside the courtyard and the gardens which early in the year were white with massed snowdrops in bloom and in May were a blue haze of wild hyacinths.

In a field at the bottom of the gardens ran a little stream of clear water in which lived some rather strange small fish. One or two village boys introduced us to these creatures, and so we came with jam jars and by carefully lifting stones from the bed of the stream we caught, with our hands, little brownish-grey fish with big fins on their heads which we were told were called "snotty bullies", and tiny crayfish of similar colouring. I took these specimens to school in their jam jar of water, carried by a string handle, and presented them to the Biology mistress who was extremely interested in them. "What are they?" she asked. "We call them snotty bullies", I replied. "Ah yes, bull fish", she said with the glimmer of a smile, and showed them to the class. The little stream is still there, gliding and rippling across the field, but where are the snotty bullies and the crayfish? Perhaps they still hide under the stones.

Just before the outbreak of the Second World War Father Fleming became too ill to stay at Dodding Green and went to live with his sister in the north-east, moving eventually to Ambleside where he died in 1945.

His successor at Dodding Green was Father Kershaw, a younger man who was often to be seen briskly walking the two-and-a-half miles to Kendal and walking the return journey too. We knew that Catholic priests did not get married and it was said by some that they were not even allowed to look at women. However, that did not mean that we could not look at him, and what we saw was a serious but not unkind face, pale, with a blue jowl, very dark eyes and hair, all of which was summed up by the seventeen- and eighteen-year-old females as being handsome. And there the admiration and the comments had to stop.

But we could and did dream of tall, dark, handsome men. They were there on the cinema screen and looking out at us from the pages of the film magazines which we read avidly and from which we cut out pictures of our favourites, pasting them into a scrapbook.

Village characters were real, however, and all around us. Perhaps we ourselves were thought of as characters by our neighbours? Aunties would certainly come into that category as two quiet, gracious little ladies, pleasant to everyone but just a tiny bit aloof, so tiny a bit that you didn't notice it.

CHAPTER FOURTEEN

Illnesses and Remedies

The usual infectious diseases amongst children almost passed us by. The most serious, scarlet fever, was contracted by Zelia but I was too young to remember much about it except that favourite soft toys, once taken to the sanatorium, were not allowed home again. But of measles, mumps and chickenpox I knew nothing until I was in my teens. As a child therefore, colds, coughs, ear-ache, tummy-ache, tooth-ache, cuts and bruises were our commonest complaints and there were remedies for them all.

The common cold, with very often an accompanying cough, was treated by a variety of hot and soothing drinks, usually at bed time. Blackcurrant tea was popular – it was made by pouring hot water onto a big spoonful of home-made blackcurrant jam in a cup, and after being drunk the currants were spooned up from the bottom of the cup and eaten. Not so pleasant was licorice water, made with hot water and hard licorice like tiny lumps of coal. More mysterious was a posset. My grandmother, Mammam, occasionally made us a treacle posset. As far as I know (for I never actually saw it made) this was hot milk, black treacle and sugar. An adult version had the addition of rum, whisky or brandy. Chests were rubbed with camphorated oil from small glass cylindrical bottles with a cork, and my mother once had a fad for me wearing an 'Iodine Locket' on a ribbon round my neck. It was round and made of Bakelite, perforated all over and stuffed with something like compressed cotton wool impregnated with iodine. It turned the skin and underclothes yellow and was a great embarrassment at school when we stripped off to vest and knickers for gym. The 'Iodine Locket' was supposed to prevent colds along with a daily dose of Kepler's codliver oil and malt.

There were other eccentric health fads. When on holiday at Allonby we would go to nearby Silloth and be taken for a walk through the pine woods. Here we were instructed to breathe deeply and inhale the pine-scented odour. Even more bizarre was to inhale the fumes of boiling tar if we happened to walk near to road-mending operations. What other noxious chemicals we also inhaled can only be imagined.

If we bruised ourselves the injured place was rubbed with a lump of soft butter. If a wasp or bee happened to sting us then we were dabbed with a 'Blue Bag', which was a small round block of blue earth pigment encased in a thin cotton bag with a little wooden handle and used on washing day to make the white clothes look whiter. Nettle stings were rubbed with dock leaves to the old jingle, "nettle sting in, docken rub out". Wet feet demanded a soaking in a mustard bath – the small galvanised tin tub in front of the fire – and for toothache bi-carbonate of soda, or if you had it in the medicine chest, a dab of cloves which smelled lovely but tasted awful.

Laxatives were legion: brimstone and treacle, castor oil, senna tea made from senna pods, syrup of figs, and as a last resort soap injections. We ran a mile from any of them though we had no objections to drinking a glass of fizzy Andrew's or Eno's fruit salts.

A warm flannel (usually a piece from a worn out woollen vest) was a great comfort for ear-ache or tummy-ache. Our parents and relatives had their own remedies. A bread poultice to 'draw' boils consisted of thick pieces of bread soaked in hot water, wrapped in a cloth and then clapped onto the affected area. For bad backs and other aching joints there was embrocation, either good old turpentine or oil of wintergreen (disguised in proprietary brands such as Sloane's Liniment) all of which could be smelled for miles around. My father frequented the local herbalist, and 'Fiery Jack' was one of his favourite preparations for aches and pains of which he had his share. My grandparents were great believers in layers of 'Thermogene' wool, worn round the body amongst the underclothes and also rather smelly. Tonics were fashionable with the ladies. Yeast tablets ('Yeast-vite'), Slippery Elm Food, Wincarnis Tonic Wine, – and Sanatogen which was taken religiously every day by little Auntie Sally.

ILLNESSES AND REMEDIES

Upset tummies, or acidosis as one of my aunts used to refer to it, were usually caused by guzzling too much honey or too many chocolates, Tunis cake at Christmas being one of the chief offenders. After vomiting several times I would lie on the sofa under a rug – feeling very sorry for myself – until it gradually passed off and an interest in food returned, – dry toast and weak sweet tea for starters, progressing to my top favourite, fried ham. Then my mother knew that recovery was complete.

Adults convalescing treated themselves to Calves Foot Jelly which was spooned from a tall, unusually shaped jar and which was anything but cheap and in my opinion was completely tasteless. My adult relatives were far from being dim-witted but it amazes me how they fell for the claims of most of these patent medicines. Perhaps they were cheaper than a consultation with the doctor and a bottle of his prescribed medicine made up by Miss Bond, pince-nez on the end of her nose, in a cubby-hole just off the waiting room at the surgery in Maude Street.

One family in the village was permanently afflicted by deafness and several members of it were deaf-and-dumb. As children we were not told, and it did not occur to us, that the reason these people could not speak was because they could not hear. They were called Thewlis and lived for a time next door to Aunties. Auntie Mary could communicate with them by using sign language, and as some of them worked under my father at the Mill he too had to be able to communicate. So I learned the deaf-and-dumb alphabet at a very early age and often 'talked' to my father and to Aunties in this way as an interesting exercise. We really did not think of this family as being any different to ourselves. They were just people who could not speak and who could not hear, apart from that they went about their business in much the same way as everyone else. The impact of this great disability just did not strike us. Many years later, after I had married and left home, my father had to have major surgery. We went into Kendal to visit him and found ourselves on the bus with Emma Thewlis who had worked for him at the Mill. Not knowing that I understood sign language she 'wrote' in the air with her finger, "How is Ted?" To her surprise I was able to reply in the manner which she understood.

For some months in the early 1930s the District Nurse lived with us at School House as a paying guest. Not that my mother needed to have paying guests but it would appear that the authority responsible felt that our family, and the amenities in our home, were suitable for such a person as Nurse Vass and her white West Highland terrier, Sheila.

Jean Jessie Vass came from Rogart in the north of Scotland. It was a romantic-sounding place but as remote to us as Russia (though our Grandpa Helliwell had once been offered a job in Russia). She was about thirty, tall and very straight, with dark hair and rosy cheeks, pleasant and kind but one knew instinctively not to try any funny tricks with her. She rode a motor bike when she first came to us and sometimes I was allowed to go with her on her rounds. I rode on the pillion and her leather maternity bag was strapped onto the carrier behind me.

Very soon the motor bike was exchanged for a little car and I went with Nurse – for this is what we called her – to outlying farms to visit mothers and their new babies. A new baby cost a hundred pounds so I was told, and I had no reason to question this. It did seem an enormous amount of money, but a baby was such a marvellous thing perhaps at a hundred pounds it wasn't too expensive. The cost must have impressed me for on one visit to Mrs Todd, a farmer's wife, I was permitted to see the mother and baby and after inspecting the infant I asked Nurse and Mrs Todd, "Did this baby really cost a hundred pounds?" "Yes, a hundred pounds; so you have to save up," said Nurse in her attractive Highland accent.

It was Nurse who introduced us to the Haggis. When she returned to School House after spending New Year in Sutherlandshire with her family she brought us a Haggis. My mother cooked it according to her instructions and my father carried it – though I have to say that it was not piped – into the dining room on a silver salver. I do not think that we were greatly impressed by it but we were pleased to have the experience of eating a genuine example of the Scots' national dish. Very sadly about ten years later Nurse was killed in a dreadful road accident between Skelsmergh and Selside.

Another paying guest for a few months was a school teacher, Miss Bakewell, which we thought was a very funny name as our mother often made Bakewell Tarts. She taught for a time at the village school. The introduction of these women into our home, even for only a short time, probably did us a world of good. Our parents were over indulgent with us, in fact we were more than a little spoiled. To have other intelligent and cultured women around us, whose professions demanded discipline and who were themselves an authoritative presence, curbed our reckless and some-times wild behaviour.

CHAPTER FIFTEEN

Outdoor Games

Before I was allowed to go outside the gates of School House alone, the back garden was my outdoor play area as a small child. My mother could keep her eye on me either from the dining room, the kitchen or the back door of the house.

Two things occupied my life out of doors in those early years. One was the swing, and the other my dolls, their pram and the centuries-old game of "houses". The swing, made by my father, had a thick, broad, wooden seat and was fastened by very heavy ropes to a branch of the tree which grew at one side of the steps leading up to the back door. Here I would sit and swing for hours, and while swinging I sang, not well-known tunes and songs but long stories to tunes which I made up as I went along. Heaven knows not only if they made sense but how they sounded. My mother, of course, thought that it was all lovely.

If I wasn't singing and swinging then I was playing houses, probably with a village friend. The back garden was enclosed by a dry-stone wall, where tiny ferns and flowering creepers grew from the crevices between the stones. One corner was set aside for the house. Usually we had a collection of old pieces of crockery and baking tins salvaged from the dustbins or the local rubbish tip. However, if our stock of pots showed signs of depletion we went round the village knocking on the doors of specially selected houses and asking, "Have you any old pots, please?" This often brought forth something, and I well remember being given certain Staffordshire flat-back chimney pieces and items of ruby glassware, slightly damaged, which would now have a place in an antique shop window.

We filled the baking tins with soil and water mixed to the right consistency, and decorated these mud pies and cakes with pebbles and brightly-coloured flower heads, and we asked each other out to tea, with our prams full of dolls, teddy bears and golliwogs.

THE GREEN LANES

The rough roads, paths and woodlands were no places for smart shoes. Indeed Uncle Tom Hackett's father, who was a country postman and walked everywhere on his delivery rounds, wore out the soles and heels of a pair of boots every week, so that one pair was always at the cobbler's while the other pair was in use. Almost all village children wore clogs, ourselves included, though ours were without irons on the toes and heels. The strap across the instep fastened with a button and was so stiff that we needed a little button-hook to secure it. And a button-hook was used to fasten the many buttons on the soft leather gaiters I wore in the winter.

My clogs were sometimes employed as a weapon against my sister. If she taunted or teased me I went for her, not tooth and nail – though I had been known to bite and scratch – but with a volley of kicking with my clogs. Indentations on the door from the dining room to the hall, made with the clogs where I vented my exasperation after Zelia had escaped upstairs, were visible up to the time when my mother left the house, and for all I know may still be there.

When at last I was considered old enough and sensible enough to be allowed outside the perimeter of School House and its gardens, I had the whole wide-open world to explore and to play in. The games we played were legion, and were all entered into with an enormous amount of energy and enthusiasm. There were no distractions during school holidays, apart from the wireless, and I took little notice of that unless the weather was bad. Even in term time (when I was driven early to bed) as soon as homework was finished I changed out of school uniform into old clothes and dashed out to join the others, who never had homework.

Our outdoor games were built around the terrain surrounding the village, woods, hills and fields, which lent themselves admirably to Hide-and-Seek, Give-a-Signal, climbing trees, exploring down the steep gorge to the river, and more sedately, bird-nesting and gathering wild flowers.

The rough unmetalled roads were totally unsuitable for roller-skating, or indeed for much activity with bicycles, but were ideal for Booly Hoops and Four-Wheels-and-a-Board.

These two latter pursuits were mainly indulged in by village boys. Girls played Whip and Top, or Diabolo. We all had Yo-Yo's and could execute a variety of fancy tricks with them. But skipping and singing games were favourites with both sexes of all ages. Some of us had individual skipping ropes with painted wooden handles and of course ours were the most elaborate and most expensive of all, some of them really did have bells on.

Boys produced long lengths of heavy rope, and with two of them turning it several of us could jump into and out of the turning rope at a time. And when it was turned at great speed and cracked as it hit the ground we skipped what was called a pepper.

The jingles we sang and the singing games we played had been handed down by our mothers and their mothers through many generations. These games were usually played by girls. Boys thought such games were soft, but there were occasions when they could be persuaded to join in. One of our favourites was, "In and out the windows".

> "In and out the windows,
> In and out the windows,
> In and out the windows
> As you have done before".

Here we joined hands, held high in a circle, with one girl weaving her way in and out and under the joined hands as we walked slowly around. Then she stood in the centre of the ring while we sang:

> "Turn and face your lover,
> Turn and face your lover,
> Turn and face your lover
> As you have done before".

She turned and faced one of the girls, or if the boys were taking part she faced one of them, and it became much more exciting as we sang, "Take her by the hand," and so on and finally, "Follow her to London," where we all trooped off, following the chosen couple.

Another singing game was:

> "The wind, the wind, the wind blows high,
> The rain comes scattering from the sky.
> She is handsome she is pretty,
> She is the toast of London city.
> She goes a courting with one, two, three,
> Pray and tell me who is she?"

Again we joined hands in a circle and moved in a clockwise direction while one girl on the outside of the circle moved in the opposite direction. When the singing reached, "Pray and tell me who is she," she touched someone on the shoulder and they ran round the circle in opposite directions to reach the vacant place. The last one to reach it remained on the outside for the next round.

> "I wrote a letter to my love
> And on the way I dropped it.
> One of you has picked it up
> And put it in your pocket.
> Was it you...you...you?"

And again a circle was formed, with one girl on the outside moving in the opposite direction and dropping a handkerchief behind someone's back, and then the race for the empty place, and so on. There was also "Nuts in May" and "Ring a Roses", "The Farmer's in his Den", and many others.   When my mother and Mammam shook the newly washed blankets in the garden they sang as they tossed the blankets up and down:

> "Shake the bed,
> Shake the bed,
> Turn the blankets over".

and here they actually turned them over as they tossed them.

OUTDOOR GAMES

My mother used to sing as she rocked me on her knee:

> "Sweet and low,
> Sweet and low,
> Wind of the western sea".

and:

> "Bye baby Bunting,
> Daddy's gone a-hunting".

and later:

> "Nancy Pancy lived in a Well,
> She brewed good ale for gentlemen.
> Gentlemen came every day,
> Till Nancy Pancy ran away".

When I was older and wanted more excitement and was allowed to stay out until after dusk, we played Hide-and-Seek, and Give-a-Signal. This was a game where we all went to hide in different places, except the one who was 'it'. After a few minutes when all were hidden, she or he would sing out loudly, "Give a Signal", and some small noise or song would be heard from around and about, until someone's hiding place was discovered.

It could all be breathtakingly exciting as dusk was falling and the blue wood-smoke curled from the cottage chimneys as the evening fires were stoked up and the first lights twinkled in the windows and the North Star appeared. Even my mother's voice calling me in after dark could not dampen the exhilaration of the chase among the woods, and the suspense of who would win and who would lose.

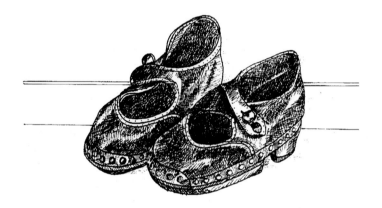

CHAPTER SIXTEEN

Food

Good food was high on my mother's list of priorities. The best food she could afford, and plenty of it, was her passport to good health. There were no dire warnings in those days to eat foods high in polyunsaturates and low in cholesterol, or prevent your arteries being blocked by keeping off dairy produce. We swallowed an abundance of milk, cream, butter, eggs, bacon and ham, beef and pork. Chicken was considered invalid food and was rarely on our table. Margarine we had never heard of until the War. Home-made bread, fruit pasties, Eccles cakes, Madeira cakes, coconut cakes and rich puddings were our daily fare. My sister and I both drank a pint of milk and a penny tub of cream every day.

The fish van called on Tuesdays, and so on that day it could be either plaice, hake or halibut for tea. Less aristocratic fish, cod, haddock, herring and the like, were unknown to us until I was once allowed to help Auntie Fanny to gut and pickle herrings in vinegar.

Tea at home was High Tea; as I have said, fish on Tuesdays, fried with bread and butter. Other days we might have a boiled egg and toast, or Skipper's sardines on toast, or perhaps an omelette. There were always biscuits or an apple to nibble, or a slice of bread and jam between meals. Surprisingly not one of the family was overweight. If we refused to eat what was provided we were threatened with prison fare, which we were assured – and sincerely believed – was dry bread and water.

Breakfast consisted of oatmeal porridge in winter, followed by bacon, egg, fried bread and tomatoes and sometimes fried beetroot. In summer we had cereals with milk and sugar. Breakfast cereals were just becoming popular and there were often two or three different brands in the kitchen at once. "Force" was advertised by Sunny Jim, and a number of packet tops sent away could bring a soft toy of him through the post. There was Puffed Wheat, Puffed Rice, and Post Toasties rather like today's cornflakes. Great were the manufacturers' inducements printed on the packets to send for this and that and so buy their products.

Succulent pork pies and other pork products were bought in Kendal from a very busy and popular shop. The two men who owned the shop were tall, fair-haired, pink-faced and sported little fair moustaches. They had pink hairy arms, and not only resembled one another (they were brothers) but, I privately thought, bore a striking resemblance to pigs as well. But my mother often made her own pies, a large standing pork pie which would feed six or eight people if we were having visitors to a pie-and-salad tea. On one occasion eight of us were seated at the table, having been served with a generous helping of pie and salad. No sooner had we started eating than my father addressed my mother: "Myrtle," he said, "what liquid have you put into this pie?" "Why," said my mother, "the usual, vinegar." "It doesn't taste like vinegar to me," said my father, "show me the bottle you took it from." So my mother opened the cupboard and took out the bottle, which was unlabelled. Father uncorked it and sniffed the contents. "This isn't vinegar," he announced, "it's whisky." We teased my mother for many weeks about the whisky pie.

Bearing in mind the pork butchers, was it my lively and fertile imagination which likened the ruddy countenance of our regular weekly butcher to one of his joints of beef? My mother always bought the same cut, Aitch bone, and Sunday dinner was roast beef and Yorkshire pudding, this latter was always served in the traditional Yorkshire manner as a separate course before the meat and vegetables. There was no set time for this meal. It might be ready at 12.30pm or it might be 2.30pm. It all depended on what time my mother started to prepare it. If there was a long gap between breakfast and dinner we filled up a corner with a slice of bread and jam. Bread and dripping was a favourite with some people, but not with me. Most of the bread we ate was home-made. It was kept in tall, brown earthenware pots called panchions which were kept under the kitchen dresser. One panchion would hold several large loaves.

A big joint of ham or gammon might be boiled in an enamel jam pan over the dining room fire, but by-and-large all my mother's cooking and baking was done on a paraffin stove and oven. It was not until after 1945 that she was able to have an electric cooker.

Cheese, toasted in front of the fire on the end of a long wire fork, was a favourite of my father and me. Some of our toasting forks were hand-made and I loved to hold the cheese until it bubbled and became brown, knowing just when to turn it round before it dripped into the fire. Holding it in front of the flames was no good, the fire had to be red and flame free otherwise the cheese just became black and smoky. Bread dipped in hot tasty gravy from the roast beef was also a favourite. We also put sugar on most things. We put it on porridge, on cereals, on fruit, on tomatoes, on puddings, we even made sugar sandwiches.

Potatoes and vegetables and soft and hard fruits if not grown in our own garden were always available for a few pence from one of the neighbours. My father grew potatoes, and when the time came round for buying the seed there was great deliberation over which variety to buy. Arran Pilot usually won the day. We had blackcurrant bushes but picking the fruit and topping and tailing them was a trial. Aunties grew gooseberries and raspberries in their little back garden and never failed to be able to make a saucer pie, from the first gooseberries of the season, for my father's birthday on the twentieth of May.

There was wild produce to be gathered in season. Mushrooms grew in a particular field between the Appleby road and the railway line, near to the Stocks. This was known as the Lily Field, where small, pale, wild daffodils blew and nodded very early in the Spring. Horse mushrooms were to be found in the ploughed fields around Patton Hall Farm, and we were introduced to these by the Parker boys whose father was the farmer there.

Blackberrying also was a serious business. Paddy Lane was the venue and the most luscious fruits actually grew on the railway embankment where we had gathered cowslips and primroses earlier in the year. Aunties took part in these expeditions, Auntie Fanny came up from Kendal and my father joined us at the weekends. We carried the blackberries in wooden chip baskets lined with brown paper. Aunties filled the lading can with them, and we took walking sticks to pull forward branches of fruit which would otherwise be out of reach.

When the fruit was brought home the jelly making began. Our jelly-bag hung from a hook in the ceiling of the cellar and dripped into a big brown-and-cream earthenware bowl. Crab apples received similar treatment. Aunties were the experts in the making of crab apple jelly with its clear pinky-golden colour and its sharp, tangy flavour which was perfect spread on their crunchy, brown buttered scones.

In September when damsons from the Lyth Valley appeared in Kendal market my father would walk there with what he called his game bags. These were deep, two-handled bags made of a type of split-cane. They were pliable and very strong, but it must have been a great drag on the shoulders to carry them the two-and-a-half miles home again, each bag containing a quarter of a stone of damsons.

Then out would come the jam pan and my mother would spend an afternoon making the fruit into jam over the fire, skimming off the stones and the scum with a slotted spoon onto a big soup plate in the hearth, then pouring the crimson purple liquid jam into hot jars and tying greaseproof paper over the tops.

We had been carefully taught from our earliest youth which fruits and berries were poisonous, and nothing would have induced us to touch them. We knew the difference between edible mushrooms and inedible toadstools, and between water cress and "dead tongue". We sucked the sweetness from clover stems and gathered deliciously sweet little wild strawberries. We went on nutting expeditions when the hazelnuts were ripe. And thus the bounty of the countryside was harvested and its goodness consumed and enjoyed.

CHAPTER SEVENTEEN

Winter Festivals

One of the exciting events of the winter was Bonfire Night, or Plot Night as Mammam called it. Outside the garden walls, at the back of School House, was a piece of waste ground between the school playground on one side and the woods on the other. From the garden wall it stretched some eighty yards before falling steeply down to the river. It was on this piece of ground that the November the Fifth bonfire was built each year.

For weeks beforehand we had trailed sticks and branches to build the bonfire. Anything else that would burn was dragged along on the four-wheels-and-a-board (known for this purpose as the Bogie), culminating the night before the Fifth with all the discarded furniture and garden refuse being brought from around the village.

It was party night at home. Aunties, Auntie Fanny and Uncle Tom were invited to see the bonfire and the fireworks, and then to have supper at School House. Each year Auntie Fanny and Uncle Tom brought with them a box of Standard fireworks which had cost half a crown. This was a very generous gift, for the box contained a splendid selection. My father provided the rockets, and with money I had been given I bought my own favourites, Roman Candles, Vesuvius Fountains, Catherine Wheels, Snowstorms, and Jack in the Box.

My father was in charge of lighting the bonfire, and all the village came out to watch. Once it was well alight we had the fireworks. "Light the blue touch-paper and retire immediately". We were very much in awe of this dire warning and stood well away as my father and Uncle Tom did the lighting. The jumping crackers jumped, the Little Demons banged, the Pin Wheels spun on the clothes post, and when the last rocket had showered its stars the grown-ups went indoors for a hot supper. We had already put potatoes into the glowing edge of the fire, and now we poked them out with a long stick. They were blackened on the outside but hot and fluffy inside, and we rushed into the kitchen for lumps of butter and cheese to put in them. Then there were parkin pigs, gingerbread men, and Plot toffee.

The following morning I was out before anyone else, searching for and picking up the spent fireworks and the rocket sticks, and my father couldn't resist coming with me and poking about amongst the still smouldering remnants of the fire. Many years later he confessed to us that he had always felt an almost irresistible urge to set fire to dry grass and woodland – an urge which, of course, always had to be stifled. No doubt the lighting of the annual bonfire gave him some satisfaction.

After the excitement of Bonfire night had faded there was Christmas to look forward to. By the end of November my mother was busy making Christmas cakes and puddings. The mixture for the puddings was put into enamel basins which had metal lids and a gadget on the lid which when twisted, tightened it onto the basin. They were then boiled for what seemed an interminable length of time in a jam pan of water over the fire.

Aunties made neither cakes nor puddings. I suppose the effort required to stir large, heavy quantities of fruit, flour, sugar and eggs was too much for them. However, Auntie Fanny not only made cakes and puddings but mincemeat as well. This went into dozens of mince pies, the tops of which were liberally covered with sugar.

So Christmas, for the most part, meant presents, parties, and special food and drink. The religious festival was acknowledged but not paramount in our celebrations. We knew the true Christian meaning of Christmas and never once doubted it. We accepted it as fact. There was no Chapel service unless Christmas Day fell on a Sunday. If there was a Church service we were unaware of it.

Three or four of us went round the village carol-singing. We sang "Away in a Manger", and "While Shepherds watched", and perhaps a verse of "Hark the Herald" – as it was always referred to – but it was a half-hearted effort. I was the only one who knew all the words, and in spite of taking a hymn book with me my companions, who had been press-ganged into going anyhow, would join in the first verse and then tail off and gradually give up altogether. More rousing was the sing-song around Aunties' harmonium where at least we had the music and we all knew the words.

Christmas presents, or "boxes" as they were called, were given to the dustbin men on their last collecting day before the Bank Holiday. There were two men, and they each received a shilling. The postman, whose morning delivery was made by bicycle, fared even better. He received half a crown and a glass of whatever was on tap on Christmas morning, because of course there was a normal delivery of post on Christmas Day.

We were a small family and did not give lavish presents all round, but as children we received gifts from our parents, from Mammam, and from the immediate Aunts and Uncle. The gift I looked forward to most of all was Teddy Tail's Annual (from Teddy Tail, the strip cartoon in the Daily Mail), and this was my father's special present to me. Mother and father together bought us a joint present. Those which I remember particularly well were a small wind-up gramophone, and a ciné film projector. We had an inkling that we were to receive a gramophone, and on Christmas morning we were awake at two o'clock, playing one of the records, which was "El Relicario". But not for long. Gramophone and records were soon impounded until a more civilised hour.

The following year the gift of the film projector was no secret. We went with our father, a week or two before Christmas, to Townley and Taylor's toyshop in Kendal to choose it. The proprietor of the shop was a small, dark man with a big black moustache. Unfortunately he also had a cleft palate. He was, however, most helpful and obliging and nothing was too much trouble for him. We naughty girls were forced to have silent mirth as this poor man invited us into the demonstration room with, "Hep horward", and explained the machines to our father. "Hiss machine hakes hifteen heet of hilm, and hiss one hakes hirty heet of hilm". All three of us had a natural talent for mimicry, and our renderings of that visit to the toyshop brought forth far more laughter than the Charlie Chaplin films we watched on our new projector.

Christmas Day followed the same pattern every year. After breakfast and the giving and receiving of the presents, which had been assembled around the tree, my mother cooked a gargantuan dinner for midday. This was always roast pork, apple sauce, home-made stuffing, roast potatoes and plenty of vegetables, followed by Christmas pudding and rum sauce. Extra chocolates and sweets were ordered from our grocers in Kendal. Round, thin wooden boxes of crème-de-menthe-flavoured Turkish Delight, a four-pound box of Meltis assorted chocolates, dates and figs in boxes lined with paper lace and which also contained a two-pronged bone fork with which to handle the fruit. And there was Tunis cake, a tall sponge cake with a very thick layer of solid chocolate on the top. Tunis cake came in a shiny, white cardboard box with a suitable Eastern scene pictured on the lid.

We hardly had time to recover from the pork and pudding when we had to put on our best frocks and go in a taxi to Castle Garth to tea, another splendid repast, with our Aunts and Uncle Tom.

Mitchell's taxi to Kendal cost three shillings on a normal day, but on Christmas Day the price went up to five shillings. Belisha Beacons had recently been introduced into the traffic regulations, and as we approached them going into Kendal I expounded on whether the name Belisha (after Mr Hore-Belisha, the Minister of Transport) was pronounced Beleesha or Belisha (as in Elisha the prophet), and I said to the driver who on this occasion was old Mr Sammy Mitchell, "What do you call them, Mr Mitchell, Beleesha or Belisha?" To which he replied in an irritated voice, "I call 'em a bloody nuisance", and that silenced me for the rest of the journey.

I loved to go to Auntie Fanny's for Christmas tea. The big oval dining table would be set with the rosebud china, and on each plate were several wafer-thin slices of Auntie Fanny's speciality, beef and ham roll, with a selection of home-made chutneys and piccalilli. There was bread and butter, teacakes, scones, currant pasty, dark sticky ginger-bread, chocolate cake with butter-cream filling, hot sugary mince pies, and jellies. The tea-making ceremony was curious. Even though there were large teapots in the house, two tiny teapots were used, and these were filled and re-filled, over and over again, from the kettle on the dining room fire and the electric kettle in the kitchen. There were two jugs on the table, one containing cream from the top of the milk, and the other containing milk which was, presumably, that from which the cream had been removed.

We had crackers and paper hats, and after the left-over food was cleared away there was a box of indoor fireworks. It was an insoluble mystery how a tiny pill, put into a tumbler of water, could turn into a mass of flowers, or how another similar pill, once touched with a lighted match, would grow into a snake.

Aunties were in residence already, having arrived at Castle Garth on Christmas Eve, and after the tea things were washed up the women withdrew into the sitting room for a good gossip. My father, Uncle Tom, Zelia and I stayed in the dining room and played either Bagatelle or card games. The visit ended with more cups of tea and Christmas cake for the grown-ups, but cold water for me in my favourite china beaker decorated with black cats. Then there were carols round the piano before the taxi took us home at nine o'clock.

New Year's Day was a Bank Holiday and that meant another day off work for my father. However, due to the local superstition that on New Year's Day the first person to cross the threshold must be a dark man, my father, being more fair than dark, was not allowed to leave the house and come into it again. It was bad enough if you inadvertently allowed a fair man over the door step, but for a fair-haired woman to enter the house it was enough to make the roof fall in, and no doubt it would have done so if we had run into Aunties and back again as we were always so eager to do. We were thus all imprisoned within the house, waiting for our dark-haired milkman. With so many thresholds to cross, and so many glasses of wine to drink on the way, he was understandably always late.

John Atkinson, the milkman, really was very dark. He was also very kind and quietly spoken. He drove a pony and trap with the milk churns rattling in the trap, and he measured out the milk from a tin pint measure into my mother's jugs. And after the formality of entering the house, and wishing us all a Happy New Year over a glass of wine, he went on his way and we were all released from bondage.

CHAPTER EIGHTEEN

Friends

Our home, with our mother in it, was of course the most vital and important thing in our lives. She was there when we left it in the morning to go to school, and there when we flung open the doors – for the doors were never locked – on our return. If by some slender chance we did not see her the minute we entered the house, we were devastated. Where was she? We ran about calling for her, upstairs, into the garden and down to the cellar; we ran to Aunties to see if she was there, but that was unlikely anyhow. But she was never more than a few yards away, and when she appeared we could relax and throw down our satchels of books and flop about before tea and the serious business of the evening began.

Aunties, too, were always there and I, particularly, ran between the two homes many times a day if only for a few minutes, and was welcomed with such quiet and gentle warmth and affection – there was no effusive hugging and kissing – that one knew instinctively the pleasure the visits gave both to them and to me. Even if the time I spent there was fleeting I would soon be rushing in again.

We had no really close friends in the village. Girls of Zelia's age were all at work – either at the Mill or in Kendal – while she was still at school, and this illustrated a wide educational and social gap. I had plenty of playmates in the village of my own age, the favourite amongst them being the already mentioned Muriel, whose Roman Catholicism took her to a different Church and to a different school and activities in Kendal. Most of our friends came from Kendal High School, and because it drew its pupils from a very wide area our main contact with them was in term-time and not during the holidays. However, some of my closest friends came from much further afield.

In her youth my mother's greatest friend was Edith Mitchell, who like my mother herself was an only child and who lived at Lees, a village near to Oxenhope. Together they travelled on the train to the girls' grammar school at Keighley and spent much of their leisure time together. My mother used to say that they were 'closer than sisters'.

Edith came to stay with my parents at School House for their house-warming party in 1920. This was a customary and traditional event held a year after a newly-married couple had taken up residence in their chosen home. And it was at this party that Edith met David Long, brother to the organ and tennis playing 'Auntie' Bessie who lived at Scarfoot Cottages between Mealbank and Laverock Bridge. Eventually they became engaged, though Edith's mother had stated that at thirty years of age she was "too young to be engaged". Fortunately however she was not deterred by this ludicrous remark and they were married in 1923.

They were both university graduates and had become Quakers, and after serving in the Friends' Ambulance Unit in the First World War – and being awarded the Croix de Guerre – David was appointed Maths master at Ackworth Quaker School. They had two sons, Michael, the elder, being six months older than myself, and Andrew four years younger. Even though we were not related they were Auntie and Uncle to us, just as my parents were to their boys.

Some part of every school holiday saw them staying at Uncle David's old home at Scarfoot Cottages with his two sisters Auntie Bessie and Auntie Hannah. Everyone was either Auntie and Uncle or Mr. and Mrs. in those days, whether you were blood relatives or not. Christian names were only used by people of the same generation and then only between relatives and close friends.

And so from my earliest recollections Michael, Andrew and myself were as brothers and sister, and spent all our holiday time together while they were staying in the area.

Sometimes I went with them when they returned home to Ackworth. The house which they occupied was at the bottom of the great garden within the school grounds and was known as Ivy Cottage. It was an old house of great character and its large rooms were tastefully and comfortably furnished with antique chairs, tables and sofas, and vases of flowers on the old oak kists. The school was, of course, on holiday and therefore empty, and so we had the complete freedom of the grounds and the gardens, the playing fields and the swimming baths. We roller-skated on the Green, which wasn't green at all but smooth tar macadam. We played cricket and football on the sports fields and we swam in the baths, the floor of which was patterned in black and white tiles measuring a yard square, and we would see how many squares we could swim across.

Auntie Edie and Uncle David had a maid who lived in. Her first job in the morning was to get up and light the kitchen fire to boil the kettle and make a pot of tea to take up to Auntie Edie in bed. I expect she did the washing and the cleaning though I do not remember seeing her about much, but she did not do the cooking.

Auntie Edie did the cooking and made some very appetising and interesting meals often quite different to those my mother made. There was never any fried food at Ivy Cottage, so bacon and eggs and fish and chips did not appear on the menus. Instead there were salads, often at breakfast time, casseroles of vegetables, and home-made wholemeal bread cut on a board at the table by Uncle David and handed out on the prongs of a silver bread-fork. Apples were grown and of course used in many ways, and hens were kept. I remember the day that one poor hen became crop-bound, and Uncle David cut open its crop, removed the offending contents and sewed it up again, and the hen fluttered off with a great squawking, no doubt mightily relieved.

If I was there over a weekend we went to Quaker Meeting on Sunday. This was a vastly different form of worship to that which I knew in the Anglican Church and the Methodist Chapel. No minister or priest to lead the service. No liturgy. No impromptu prayers. No Bible reading. Maybe a familiar hymn, but mostly there was silence, broken only by a voice perhaps reciting a poem or part of one, I particularly remember on one occasion a high-pitched voice which could have been male or female calling, "Hey nonny nonny, hey nonny nonny," and I could not help wondering what it all meant, at the same time suppressing a fit of the giggles.

The time flew, and a week was over all too quickly. I returned home on the train, my brain bursting with fresh ideas of what to read next, what new interests to pursue, and though I am sure I did not identify it at the time, my spirit uplifted.

Another family, from my mother's home village of Oxenhope, were the Ratcliffes. They lived in a large detached house, built to their own specification and set in about an acre of land. It had taken a long engagement to save the large amount of money necessary to have this house built (eight hundred pounds I was told, a monumental amount), and to be able to go into it newly married. It was called Marshcotes, and like Ivy Cottage was a house of quality but much more modern, being a product of the 1920s. Its kitchen featured an Aga cooker which was an innovation in those days. The dogs sat with their backs up against it and the cats even sat on top of it.

There were three daughters in the family, the two elder being twins and slightly younger than I was. Norman Ratcliffe worked in Keighley but his heart was in the small-holding he had created on his land. He kept a cow, hens, guinea fowl and peacocks, and ponies for the girls, but his greatest interest was his bees. He took his hives out onto Haworth moors, and we at School House were often on the receiving end of jars and combs of heather honey.

Violet played the violin in the Keighley orchestra, she used to laugh about how much the overture to "Tannhauser" made them sweat, and two notable singers of the day, Muriel Brunskill and Isobel Baillie stayed at Marshcotes when they were performing in the area. The girls took violin lessons but were never sufficiently interested to make any real progress.

There had been a violin maker in Oxenhope. His name was Kershaw Barrett, and one of his daughters, a violinist herself, was a friend of my mother's. It was therefore my mother's keen wish that I should have a violin made by this man. Mrs Ratcliffe was instructed to buy one for me just prior to one of my visits to Marshcotes. When it was time for me to return home on the train I carried not only the new violin but a kitten, whose mother was one of the Marshcote cats. This pussy was completely marmalade-coloured without a trace of white in her fur, and this variety was known locally as a Chintz cat, and this was the name we gave her. A great joke was made by both families about my luggage containing the Cat and the Fiddle.

When Violet and her daughters came to visit us we met them at Kendal railway station and took them to have tea and cakes at Mr Lewthwaite's café in Finkle Street. We sat at the tea table in excited anticipation as the uniformed waitress brought the tea things and a three-tier cake stand of delectable cream cakes. Zelia and I had already been warned by our mother that we must not say, "I bags that one" when the cakes appeared. The warning was quickly forgotten – or completely disregarded – as both we and our young guests all said together, "I bags that one". We further disgraced ourselves by giggling at Mr Lewthwaite's enormous waxed moustache as he strolled majestically among the tea tables enquiring of his customers if everything was satisfactory.

And so my friends could be divided into three groups. Firstly those from school who filled and influenced my life during term-time. These girls came from a diversity of backgrounds; the daughters of shopkeepers, hoteliers, doctors, farmers, and tradesmen and craftsmen like my father. Some very firm friendships were forged and two particularly have endured for more than six decades.

The second group were my friends who lived in Yorkshire and who I only saw in the holidays. Inevitably as we grew older and the War came we went our separate ways and saw less and less of each other until we gradually lost contact altogether.

The third group were the village girls and boys. They were there all the time of course and I could become involved in their games and activities whenever I wanted and indeed organise many of them myself.

And so I was introduced and integrated into all sections of local society at a very early age. Looking back to those times I realise how fortunate I was to know and spend time in such lovely and attractive houses as my own home, Ivy Cottage and Marshcotes and to be influenced by the creative interests and good taste of their occupants, clear memories of which have remained with me all my life.

CHAPTER NINETEEN

Indoor Activities

Young mothers of the late twentieth century, whose children sit for hours in front of the television set, have seldom had to think up ways of occupying them out of school hours. Perhaps it was because my mother had been a teacher that she had plenty of constructive ideas for occupying our indoor leisure time, long before the advent of television. She taught us to read and write before we went to school, and paper and pencils, paint and crayons were never far from my busy fingers. She also, let it be said, had the wherewithal to buy drawing books, exercise books, books with pictures to crayon and to copy, and 'magic' painting books where all that was needed was a pot of water and a brush to put it on with, and the colours appeared as if by magic.

Shirley Temple – the child-star of the 1930s with her bouncing curls, dimpled cheeks and beautiful dresses – was my idol, and I played for hours with cardboard cut-out Shirley Temple dolls and a vast range of paper cut-out clothes.

Another absorbing indoor pastime was my farmyard, and as can be imagined I had every conceivable kind of animal and poultry, and fences, gates, trees, haystacks, wheelbarrow, cart, water-trough, hen-hut and cow-shed, in those days all made of hollow lead which was easily broken. But broken legs could be mended by Mammam, with match sticks, and it was quite an amusing novelty to have a carthorse with one wooden leg.

Aunties introduced me to what they called Corkwork, or what was more generally known as French Knitting. Into the top of a large empty wooden cotton reel were hammered four evenly spaced tacks around the outside. Wool from a ball was looped and knotted around each tack, and after the last tack had been so treated the cotton reel was held in the left hand (for a right-handed person) and with the right hand the wool was held above and across the loop

around the first tack, and the loop brought over the wool –
and so over the tack – with a pointed piece of wood, then
onto the next tack, and so on *ad infinitum*. The resulting
cylindrical piece of knitting was guided through the hole in
the bobbin and if one had plenty of wool, and plenty of
patience to keep at it, one could produce a snake-like length
of knitting which someone like Mammam would coil
around and stitch into a table mat. A sophisticated and
professionally manufactured French Knitting set could be
bought in a brightly coloured box, but the home-made one
was much more interesting and much more fun. These
particular indoor pastimes I indulged in alone and did not
feel the need of a playmate.

Michael and Andrew Long spent a great deal of time at
School House during their frequent holidays in the village
at Scarfoot, and together we played with a tin-plate
Hornby train-set on a small circular track. We did jig-saw
puzzles, played Ludo, Snakes and Ladders, Lexicon,
Dominoes and Draughts. On one memorable occasion
Michael and I were playing draughts on the dining table
watched by our respective fathers. I was winning, and
Michael could not find a way to stop me. His father leaned
over his shoulder and told him what move to make to get
out of trouble. I was furious and, to quote my delighted
father, "upskelled" the draughtboard and the draughts
flew all over the room. But this was an isolated incident
and the three of us were good and firm friends and played
well together. They introduced me to 'Solitaire' and to
stamp collecting, and if on the odd occasion we were
"stalled" (at a loose end), "let's do stamps" usually solved
the problem. Their mother, Auntie Edie, guided our occu-
pations along educational lines, and 'Lists' was one of her
favourite games. We each had a pencil and paper. In a column on the left-hand side of the paper we wrote, one
under the other, "Country, County, Town, Village, Book,
Play, Bird, Animal, Girl's Name, Boy's Name," and so on
until we had about twenty items. Then a letter from the
Alphabet was chosen and away we went, writing down
against the subject the answer in that particular letter.

INDOOR ACTIVITIES

The book from which I was taught to read really did have 'The Cat Sat on the Mat' in it. From there it was a short step to the *Peter Rabbit* books, and most beloved of all, *Alice in Wonderland*, *Peter Pan* and *The Wind in the Willows*. I was an imaginative child and was held in thrall by the Never-Never-Land and its inhabitants and by the adventures of Toad, whose exploits both terrified and delighted me at the same time. I believed in a world of Giants and Fairies and would not at all have been surprised if one night Tinker Bell had flown into my bedroom through the often wide-open window. Directly my mother had tucked me up for the night and had gone downstairs, I jumped out of bed, opened the curtains and threw the window up, whatever the weather. I loved to lie in bed with the clothes under my chin and look at the moon and stars, or the clouds riding by on a windy night which blew the curtains into the room and made the old cypress trees creak and groan. When mother herself came to bed she always looked in when I was fast asleep and closed the window.

I never tired of fairy tales. I read them over and over again, sighing with bliss over the happy endings of Cinderella and The Sleeping Beauty and weeping over The Little Mermaid. My first book of poems was called *For Your Delight* and was published in 1924. I had listened to Aunties reciting poems from their youth and knew them all by heart, but to be able to read for myself a whole book of new ones was enchantment:

> "Minnie and Winnie slept in a shell,
> Sleep little ladies and they slept well.
> Pink was the shell within, silver without,
> Sounds of the great sea wandered about."

This was surely what I heard – sounds of the great sea wandering about – when I put Auntie Mary's big cowrie shells to my ears. And "Wynken, Blynken and Nod one night sailed off in a wooden shoe," though all rather puzzling was nevertheless fascinating.

But the tale of The Foolish Harebell made me cry and I carefully averted my eyes from that particular page. Zelia, however, took some pleasure in frightening and taunting me, and used to quote verses from the Harebell poem on purpose to upset me, which was rather cruel, but sisters are often hurtful to each other and how I hurt her has already been revealed. She also used to sing to me the story of The Three Dragons, which I disliked intensely. Another way she struck terror into me was by telling me that under the great slabs of rock on the river bed near the Mill, which could be seen when the water was low, there were giants buried. I truly believed it, and if I was alone I ran along the particular stretch of road which overlooked that part of the river.

Other frightening things were *Strewel Peter* and ghost stories. It was 'the long-legged scissor man' of whom I was most afraid – he who cut off children's thumbs – because I too sucked my thumb. Other cautionary tales were not so worrying, though the woeful illustration of the cats crying pools of tears over the dreadful tale of Harriet and the matches had me adding my tears to theirs.

But ghosts were something different. Even though I would scream along with my friends at the mention of them I don't believe I was ever afraid of the supernatural. Some of us who have been born and bred in the hills are endowed with the gift of 'second sight'. We have a glimpse in the mind of certain things which may happen in the future or are given access to some area of a spirit world. Some members of the Robinson family have this dubious gift, Auntie Mary was one and I am another. Two unusual stories have emerged and I have no reason to believe that either of them has been embellished.

The first concerns Hole House Farm in Howgill, near to the birthplace of my father at Draw Well Farm. This farm has been occupied for over one hundred and fifty years by various members of the Robinson and Metcalfe family, and at the time of writing its owner is my second cousin. There is an old tale about a little coloured servant being murdered there many years ago. Following this the chains outside the house were heard to rattle and things were seen in the night in a certain room. Granny Robinson dismissed these tales, and being an unimaginative woman volunteered to sleep alone in the haunted room. She related afterwards that during the night she awoke and something appeared from out of one corner of the room, came over to her bed, and returned to the corner.

The other story concerns my father and was told to me by him. He was nine years old when his father died and not long afterwards he had been helping with haymaking at a farm some distance from his home. It had grown dark before he was fully aware of it and he set off hurriedly across the fields to walk home. After some time he realised that he was lost. He was only a little boy, his father had just died, he was alone and he was afraid. Not knowing what to do he sat down on the grass and sang the only hymn he could think of, which was "Lead Kindly Light":

> "Lead kindly light
> Amid th'encircling gloom
> Lead thou me on.
> The night is dark
> And I am far from home
> Lead thou me on."

"And then," he said to me, "someone came and took me by the hand and put me on the right path to home, but I never saw who it was." My childhood experiences of fear were infrequent and fleeting. I was a happy and healthy extrovert. I loved everything in the countryside where I was born and brought up, the garden at home, the fields and woods, streams and rivers, fells and mountains, the lanes and hedgerows, the trees and flowers, and the small wild creatures which lived there.

CHAPTER TWENTY

Walks

It was countryside which was made for walking, but no one from the village walked in it. No adults, that is to say. I suppose looking back to that time that they were all too busy. Working hours were long and included part, if not all of Saturday. What remained of the short weekend was taken up with shopping trips to Kendal, repairing bicycles, gardening and jobs round the house. No time for luxuries like walking just for pleasure, even though it was a leisure activity which did not involve any expense.

Aunties, whose quiet and uneventful lives jogged along without having to go out to work, could occasionally be persuaded to walk onto Paddy Lane and to sit on the wall near to what was once the quarry and to play 'shops' with me. This game was especially popular in the Autumn when the brown, crunchy seed-heads of the docken plant could be stripped off in handfulls and became 'brown sugar'. I, of course, was the shopkeeper, and when they asked for a pennyworth of brown sugar I pretended to weigh it out and I handed it to them on a large dock leaf.

Outsiders who came to visit village families did go for walks. Uncle Tom and Auntie Fanny often cycled up to Aunties from Kendal on a Sunday evening, and when they did so Zelia and I went for a walk with them. The route we took was always the same. Up to Hayfell bridge, across the bridge, through the gate, and into the undulating field which formed the lower slopes of Benson Knott and which was known locally as the Lots.

I carried my cricket bat and a ball. Cricket on a Sunday evening did not please the three Aunts but they would never have dared to say so in front of Uncle Tom. Auntie Fanny sat on some rocks from a tumbled-down dry stone wall, part of which also served as a wicket, and we three would play a great game of cricket, Uncle Tom slogging the ball for 'six' all around the so-called pitch.

When we tired of that we walked along the field and out through another gate onto Paddy Lane and played Hide-and-Seek in the Lord's wood. Whether the Lord had been one of the landed gentry or was indeed the heavenly Lord I learned about at Sunday School I was never sure, but I did often wonder.

Paddy Lane was our favourite walk. For much of its length the railway from Oxenholme to Carlisle ran parallel, so there were always trains to see. In the distance, looking south across the railway line, were Kendal, Scout Scar and the Lakeland Fells, and if my Uncle and Aunt felt energetic enough to walk beyond Benson Hall and up the hill, on a clear evening we could see the sea.

Paddy Lane was also, as I have mentioned earlier, the domain of Mrs Turner. When we passed the gate leading into the field where her caravan stood, and she happened to be outside it on some domestic task, my Aunt and Uncle would say, "good afternoon" or "good evening", and she would reply and maybe pass the time of day. She called everyone 'Lovie', and so became known herself as Lovie, and was always referred to in this way.

Muriel and I would sometimes stroll along Paddy Lane with the dog, and if we walked as far as the caravan we often encountered Mrs Turner. We really need not have been afraid of her. She was completely harmless and must have had her own reasons for isolating herself from society and living in this solitary manner. On one occasion she offered to show us some baby birds whose nest was in the bole of a big tree. She put her hand inside the tree and brought out several nestlings which she held in the palm of her hand to show us. Then she gave a toothless laugh and said, "Oh look, they've Ba-baa-ed on Lovie's hand!" And sure enough they had.

The Long family walked a great deal during their sojourns at Scarfoot and very often took me with them. Walking with them was largely educational and certainly botanical in flavour. The walks were also brisk and much further in distance than the slow rambles of Sunday evenings. By the time we had traversed the whole length of Paddy Lane to the Greyhound Public House (but not entered it), up the Sedbergh road and past Fisher Tarn, along the lane leading to the hamlet of Docker and down the Appleby Road to Hayfell Bridge and so back to the village, I was trailing behind, scuffing my shoes and rather fed-up with learning the Latin names of wild flowers and identifying all the surrounding hills.

I was not averse, however, to a day out walking in Lakeland with them. This meant a drive in the car and a picnic lunch, as well as the exhilaration of the modest climb over Sty Head Pass or up Helvellyn one Easter – and snowballing on the top – and to the top of Skiddaw, having lost our way and ending up scrambling on the screes.

But by far the most memorable such day out was when I was taken to Haweswater to see the new reservoir dam half-built and to learn about the imminent flooding of the valley, which included the hamlet of Mardale. At school I had been taught The Ballad of Semerwater and had listened to Debussy's *La Cathédrale Engloutie*, and here it all was, about to happen in real life. Even as a young girl I was appalled to think of people being turned out of their homes and the dead exhumed from their graves and re-buried elsewhere so that this beautiful valley could be drowned to give what came to be called "Mucky Manchester" more water.

As children, expeditions over the fields and hills and through the woods might come into the category of walks, though we never thought of them as such. It was always easier to be out and about on foot rather than on a bicycle. Cycling was alright if you were going somewhere definite, but the village roads and lanes roundabout produced too many sharp stones and thorns to be able to cycle far without having a puncture.

On some hot summer evenings we might set off through the fields to the head of the Mill race to swim, changing into our swimming costumes behind big trees and generally just splashing about in the water because there wasn't really enough room to swim more than a few strokes. On other days we might walk through Foster's Wood, a steep wooded bank above the river, to gather armfuls of bluebells and up to the farm known as Patton Hall to gather mushrooms.

Hayfell Bridge has featured many times in this account, and it is here again as a venue for trainspotting. The Long boys and I spent hours sitting on the bridge writing down the names and numbers of the locomotives which passed all day on their journeys north and south. And while there was a lull without a train – and as the signal box was just on the other side of the line we could see when a train was signalled and therefore soon approaching – I would dash across the line and pinch one or two sticks of Mrs Hutton's rhubarb, and we would see who could eat a mouthful without our faces creasing up with the sour taste.

On one memorable occasion we saw a passenger throw a small brown paper parcel from the train window. It landed on the line just below us. I would go down and retrieve it and open it. It contained several very small and neat ham sandwiches. The question was, should we eat them? After some discussion we decided that we had better not, after all why had they been thrown away if they were alright? So what to do with them? I had the bright idea of putting the parcel on one of the lines and watching the next train run over it.

The boys, less daring than myself, would have absolutely nothing to do with this prank but I again descended from the bridge, put the packet on the southbound line, and we waited and watched. It was rather disappointing. The wheels of the locomotive just knocked it to one side instead of squashing it flat or shredding it up and scattering bits of bread and ham all over the track as we had hoped. It can be noted that even though the boys would have no part in this exercise they were as interested as I was in the outcome.

So much of my earliest youth was spent out of doors. There were hardly any motorised vehicles and it was completely safe for children to wander away from home unaccompanied by adults. Small wonder then that we roamed far and wide and had our special and favourite places where we had a den, a tree house, a cave or a quiet wooded dell. Sometimes we took our dogs, sometimes we carried our dolls and sometimes, but not often, we took a picnic, which usually consisted of jam sandwiches, maybe a piece of cake, and a bottle of pop.

I don't think that my mother was very keen on packing up food for picnics – she liked to have a meal with us all sitting at the table in a civilised manner – and she would never have gone for a country walk just for the pleasure of it. The necessity of frequently having to walk to Kendal and back when either the bus did not stop because it was already full, or when there was no bus at all, would be all the walking she needed and indeed all and more than she wanted. On occasions we had to walk the two-and-a-half miles home from Kendal in the dark, either late on a winter's afternoon or perhaps after having been to the pictures. As we left behind the street lamps lighting up the last houses of Ash Meadows, and stepped off the pavement into the darkness of the unlit road, she said that it was like stepping off the edge of the world.

But for myself the countryside for ever beckoned, and my greatest pleasure was to walk in it. As the seasons came and went it was ever changing; the very nature of its undulations and the variety of its natural features invited exploration and it drew me into it like a magnet. I never tired of wandering through its friendly woods and tramping the familiar lanes and fields. I was always looking to see what was new and fresh and to see what was happening; and then, in the midst of all the eagerness, I could stand quite still and listen, and absorb the sounds and scents of earth and air.

CHAPTER TWENTY-ONE

Holidays

My father had one week's holiday from work each year. Ordinary tradesmen had no holidays in the 1930s, and if they took a Bank Holiday off work they forfeited their pay. Whether or not my father was paid I do not know. The week chosen by the Mill owners was Bank Holiday week, which was then the first week in August, and for us it meant a week at Morecambe.

The seaside was no novelty to us. The nearest point to Kendal for sea and sand was Sandside on the Kent Estuary, and a mile or so further on was Arnside, which was a bigger village and had better and safer beaches. Sandside not only had quicksand but the tide could sweep in and maroon children on the sandbanks only a few yards from the shore and safety. We often spent a day at Arnside, and it was to Arnside that we went for the Sunday School Treat. The journey was made by train and on that particular occasion we all had tea at the Green Café, which was a great thrill and something we remembered for weeks afterwards.

It was in this area of Morecambe Bay that a vessel of the Spanish Armada is said to have been wrecked, and its remaining crew cast ashore. In 1588 when the great Spanish fleet was not only routed by Drake but devastated by storms in the English Channel, those vessels which were able escaped up the east coast, braved the waters of the Pentland Firth and rounded into the Atlantic, hoping to reach Spain again. One of their number is said to have come to grief in this little area of coastline which we knew so well. When I look at photographs of my paternal grandmother as a young woman, and her daughter Elizabeth, I feel sure that their ancestors of three hundred years earlier could have been from that stricken ship.

The journey to Morecambe for our holiday was made by train, having first taken a taxi from School House to the railway station in Kendal. We also finished the journey by taxi, from the Promenade station in Morecambe to the boarding house in the West End where we would spend the week.

It was quite a usual arrangement to book rooms with service at a boarding house, for perhaps two or three guineas a week. We had two bedrooms and a private sitting room and dining room combined. We bought our own food, and the items which needed cooking – like bacon and eggs for breakfast and meat or fish and vegetables for dinner – were handed to the landlady in the evening for the following day's meals. We kept our own bread, butter, cakes, jam, fruit and biscuits in a cupboard in the sideboard and used it as we needed it. This was a very satisfactory arrangement. There was no cooking or washing up for my mother and we could choose and buy the food we wanted to eat.

Most of the day was spent out and about. If the weather was good we went onto the sands (not 'the beach' in those days), having first bought a bucket and spade, celluloid windmill and paper flags from a nearby shop. I was not allowed to have a metal spade in case, in my enthusiasm, I drove the blade of it into my bare foot. A wooden spade was a bit tame and did not produce the results a metal one would have done, but the law had been laid down and it was no use trying to alter this particular one as my mother remained implacable. Down on the shore the Punch and Judy man gave several shows a day, and we loved to watch a small group of 'Nigger Minstrels' performing on a small square wooden stage set up on the sands. They played banjos and banged tambourines and wore brightly coloured costumes. At the end of their show my father gave me sixpence to put into the cloth cap which was brought round the audience for contributions.

The very posh Midland Hotel had recently been built – in the style we now call Art Deco – and even more recently the new swimming baths. The baths were open-air and very spacious, with plenty of room not only for swimmers but spectators as well, and the amenities included a café and a restaurant. We thought the whole complex was very grand indeed, and we swam on most days with our parents watching. They did not come into the water with us – neither of them being in any way inclined towards sporting activities – and as Zelia was a good swimmer and I had not yet learned to swim I splashed about at the shallow end of the pool in a green and orange rubber tyre. The best part for me came after we were dried and dressed when we were taken to the café to have a hot drink. Zelia had Horlick's, but I always chose a Hot Chocolate – milky and frothy, very chocolaty and utterly delicious.

If it was chilly or wet we went round the shops and the amusement arcades. I had saved up my pocket money for some weeks and usually had about half-a-crown to spend. One year I bought a cardboard box with a hinged lid, covered with shells, which cost one-and-sixpence. This was a prized possession for many years. Another time I bought a little basket with a handle which had been made from a coconut. Odd pennies were spent on sweets and in slot machines and in the amusement arcades, which my father enjoyed as much as I did.

The greatest treasure from the shops in Morecambe was Shirley. I had been promised a birthday present of a full-sized pot doll for some time. We had had a big celluloid baby doll called Molly, Zelia had a Teddy, we had a golliwog and a black doll, and I had a cloth doll dressed in rose-coloured velvet and appropriately called Rosemary. But Shirley was quite different. She had brown curly hair that was short and thick, brown eyes with eyelashes, and she went to sleep. She also cost two guineas, which was very expensive at a time when a tradesman's weekly wage was about three pounds ten shillings. I loved Shirley with all my heart. I tucked her up in her pram and wheeled her about. I nursed her in my arms, and I dressed her and undressed her a dozen times a day. Some of the babies dresses and shoes which we had worn, and which mother had saved, fitted her perfectly. She filled my life for many years to come.

Other holidays were spent at Allonby on the Solway Firth. My father was not able to join us on these sojourns because he was at work, and my mother never seemed to have any qualms about leaving him alone for a week. Perhaps she knew perfectly well that she had provided for him, and that he would be able to manage. Aunties were there, of course, but I never knew why he did not go to them for meals. I had pangs of conscience at leaving him, and even though I loved to go to Allonby I was relieved to return home and to find him all right.

To get to Allonby we took the train to Penrith, and there changed onto the single track railway to Keswick and along the shores of Bassenthwaite Lake to Cockermouth. Our friends the Long family were already in Allonby, and Uncle David drove to Cockermouth to meet us and thus we completed this roundabout journey in his car.

The Longs rented Keswick Cottage, a small house facing the Green which ran the length of the village and was bisected by the busy road from Maryport to Silloth. Our family stayed at Miss Bowman's, near to Keswick Cottage, having the same arrangement as at the boarding house in Morecambe. There was Miss Bowman the Aunt, who did the cooking, and Miss Bowman the Niece, who waited at table. Both women smiled a great deal but seemed almost incapable of speech. However it was an excellent establishment and we returned there year after year.

Michael and Andrew and I spent the whole day together, and once we had been taken over the busy road – for we were not allowed to cross it alone – we had the Green, the shingle and the miles of golden sands at our disposal. I built elaborate castles in the sand, the boys built forts and Silloth Docks. We buried each others legs and feet in the sand and pretended one of us was sitting in a boat which we built up of sand around him. We played English cricket and French cricket. Sometimes the grown-ups would join us and set up a windbreak made from old blankets fastened to wooden stakes, and there the ladies sat and read, knitted and talked, and Uncle David would give a hand with the sand-building and play any game we thought up. The Longs had a resident maid, Miriam, and as she and Zelia were about the same age they were good company for one another during the evenings when Miriam's services were not required.

HOLIDAYS

Bathing was safe but Uncle David always bathed with us, and our entry into the sea was timed for an hour before a meal on days when the tide was right. "Uncle David, when are we going to bathe?" was a constant *cri de coeur* as the time for changing into our swimming costumes drew near. At high tide we played 'ducks and drakes' on the shingle or collected sea coal, bits of bleached wood, shells and pebbles, but by far the greatest attraction when the tide prevented us from being on the sands was the Putting Green, situated on the Green itself just across the road from Keswick Cottage.

In charge of the eighteen-hole course was Bob Studholme, a retired local worthy with a flat cap, a big white moustache and a weather-beaten complexion and who exuded a lovely aroma of pipe tobacco. He sat in a little hut which smelled pleasantly of wood and tobacco and from where he sold tickets (twopence a round) and dispensed the sticks, balls and score cards. We played so often, and applied ourselves so seriously to the game, that we became amazingly proficient, and even though some holes were notoriously difficult we had been known to go round the course in 38. On the rare occasions, and they were rare, when we hung about wondering what to do next, "let's have a round of putt," always solved the problem.

There were no evening entertainments except for one night a month, which happily coincided with our visit, when silent films were shown at the local Reading Room, and we had a pennyworth of chips from a mobile fish and chip van after the show. We returned home from Allonby with our legs, arms and faces the colour of the sand itself, and our hair bleached by sun and wind.

These then were the holidays we spent away from home, – a week at Morecambe, a week at Allonby and, as I have already described, a week at Oxenhope. There were my occasional trips alone to Oxenhope and to Ackworth.

We were extremely lucky. Hardly any families in the village could afford to take a holiday away from home. A day at the seaside would be their only treat.

CHAPTER TWENTY-TWO

Winter Sports

Winter weather did not deter us from being out of doors. In fact there was little inducement to stay inside. There was no central heating and the house was cold except for the living room which had a coal fire, though sitting up to it one was roasted at the front and frozen at the back for much of the time. Rain kept us indoors of course, but snow and frost saw us out and about.

The hilly fields in front of School House and Woodside Terrace were ideal for sledging. We had a good, hand-made wooden sledge, made by a joiner in the village called Billy Brown, and when the first snow fell, out came all the youngsters with their sledges. The first task was to rub the rust off the runners, and we did this by dragging the sledges up and down the snow-covered parts of the road until the runners were smooth and shiny. If the snow was crisp it didn't take long, and then we were off through the gate and into the field.

We were warmly clad in thick skirts, woolly stockings and wellingtons, with scarves, gloves and woolly hats, – no trousers for girls in those days. We trudged up to the top of the hill, which was long and steep, dragging our sledges behind us by the ropes. Once at the top one had to decide whether to go down alone, and if so whether sitting, or belly-flopper, that is to say lying flat on one's tummy on the sledge. Two or three of us might sit astride one sledge, with one of the bigger boys sitting at the back holding the rope to guide it. Alone, one almost always went down belly-flopper. The snow soon became impacted and slippery and thus the descent became progressively faster.

There was another field, off the lane between the village and Laverock bridge, to which the boys migrated when the Mealbank field became too tame. We girls followed them of course, but in spite of being willing to have a go at anything I could never bring myself to sledge down that field. It was so sickeningly steep.

THE GREEN LANES

When the winter frost was hard and prolonged the little tarn, up the hill from the village and known locally as The Reservoir, froze enough for us to skate. It was reported to be 'bearing' by those boys daring enough to step onto the ice and test its strength. That was enough and all we wanted to hear. Out came the skaters and their skates, a curious assortment of ancient and modern, some with boots, some to clip onto shoes. My father first taught us to skate, he wearing an old wooden pair from his youth. These were strapped onto shoes or boots round the feet and the ankles, but had little or no ankle support or protection. We, of course, had been bought sparkling new skates by our extravagant mother. They were screwed into soft brown leather boots, laced up to mid-calf length, and were the envy of many local girls and youths.

In a long spell of hard frost we skated every night. It was an exhilarating experience in the cold and clear air, often in bright moonlight. The railway line from Oxenholme to Carlisle ran through the field, a few yards from the reservoir, and it all added to the excitement of the night when a train came roaring out of the cutting, under Hayfell bridge and out into the open field, steaming and grinding up the steep gradient, its fire glowing and throwing off a shower of sparks. We waved to the driver and his fireman, and they waved back to us and blew their whistle.

Once an enterprising member of the gang brought a wind-up gramophone and a selection of waltzes for us to skate to, and we were even joined by skaters from Kendal. My mother made me a flared grey skirt and a purple polonecked sweater with a pattern of blackberries on it to wear, a fashion we had no doubt seen in a magazine.

In one particularly long spell of freezing weather we ventured further afield with our skates. Skelsmergh Tarn was also reported to be 'bearing', so five or six of us – our skates and boots dangling round our necks – walked some two miles up Betty Scott Lane one Saturday afternoon. The ice was wickedly slippery and glassy, and we were not half so clever as we thought we were. The most adventurous of us even went on the bus to Rydal Water and had an afternoon's skating there, but the little reservoir at Mealbank was the best of all, and when the thaw eventually arrived our life became dull, and, we asked ourselves, however would we pass the evenings?

CHAPTER TWENTY-THREE

Pets

There were always pets at School House. Grandpa Helliwell had kept guard dogs at his mill in Oxenhope – one of which was a Saint Bernard called Pilot – so my mother was used to having dogs in the home. But the first creature I remember in the house was Dick, the yellow canary. He lived in a rectangular cage in the dining room window until I was about six years old. He chirped and sang all day, all day that is until I came downstairs early one Sunday morning and found him lying on his back – dead – on the floor of his cage. Poor Dick.

Some years later my mother took a fancy for having a budgerigar, and bought a pretty pale blue one together with a much smarter cage than Dick's, full of toys, bells and mirrors to amuse this new bird whose name was Peter. My mother was sure that he would learn to talk and she said, "Hello, Peter," to him dozens of times a day, and in fact he may have made a noise which sounded like, "Hello, Peter," but unfortunately he did not live long enough to make any further utterances. He was followed by another Peter, green in colour, whose life was even shorter than Peter the First. Clearly School House was not the right environment for caged birds.

Meanwhile Zelia and I had our own pets whose living quarters were either outside or in the cellar. I can still smell the hot bran mash we fed to a black-and-white angora rabbit, which bit my finger and left a scar which is still visible, – and we had several white mice in a box-like cage with wire netting at the front.

We collected frogs' spawn from the reservoir and when the tadpoles grew into frogs we made Frog Houses from shoe boxes, complete with doors and windows. I don't think that the frogs cared very much for living in a shoe box villa and they soon escaped, no doubt looking for somewhere wetter. Zelia kept goldfish, first in a large spherical bowl on a table in the front sitting room, and then in a rectangular fish tank. When one fish died it was immediately replaced by a new one. I wasn't very interested in goldfish: they were slow, silent and uncommunicative. Dogs were much more fun.

My mother favoured Cairn terriers. One was called Fay, a fragile-looking little thing who died of distemper when quite young. It does rather seem that there was a death sentence on animals which came to live at School House. They certainly did not die of neglect; they were more likely to be killed by kindness. Fay's successor, Glen, who features elsewhere in this narrative, lived to be a very old dog and eventually just expired of old age.

Other School House residents, permanent and temporary, brought dogs with them. When Mammam and Grandpa came to live with us they brought their Yorkshire terrier, Billy. He was a good-natured and well-behaved animal and already quite old at the time of their removal to School House. One day he disappeared and was still missing two days later. Mammam and my mother were very upset and worried. We all walked the lanes and woods calling for him, but not a sign of Billy. Then on the third day, when I was up to my usual explorations in the wood bordering Cross Lane, I found him. He was whimpering and trembling all over, wet and bedraggled and with a horrid tin can tied to his tail. I picked him up and rushed home with him in my arms. What anger there was, mixed with rejoicing at his return; to think that anyone could do such a thing to a friendly, helpless creature. Perhaps if he had been less friendly and snarled and shown his teeth his persecutors might have fled without harming him.

When Nurse came to live with us she brought Sheila, her white West Highland terrier. This animal was a one-woman dog and we saw little of her; she stayed in Nurse's room while she was on her rounds on the motorbike and when Nurse graduated to a car Sheila went along with her.

Hardly in the category of domestic pets but living in the house, though separate from the humans, were the bees. They had their dwelling inside the front wall of the house and flew in and out through a hole between the limestones, just above the front door. We did not trouble them and they did not trouble us, though they were ever-present, and a great deal of bee-activity – coming and going and weaving in and out with incessant buzzing – went on in the summer months. My father was at a loss as to what to do about them. Our bee-expert friend Norman Ratcliffe from Oxenhope came over, and he and my father poked a long stick into the hole and drew it out again covered with honey. They came to the conclusion that as the bees were completely un-get-at-able, nothing could be done short of partly demolishing the wall of the house. One summer evening they swarmed on the rustic archway. There were frantic phone calls to bee-men in Kendal and one cycled out in the dusk complete with skep, helmet, gloves and other impedimenta necessary to remove the swarm. We thought, hopefully, that this might be the last we would see of the bees, but they returned and were still in residence when my mother left the house in the late 1950s.

Cats were our favourite domestic pets and they were all very long-lived, so the School House environment must have suited them. Chintz was the first, and her origins have already been chronicled. She was not spayed and so produced a vast number of kittens, all of which were drowned at birth in a bucket with a cover over it. My father hated doing it, so sometimes I did it for him though I disliked it equally, but there was no alternative. Sheba, a long-haired Persian, was another long-liver. She lost her teeth in old age and my mother then fed her on bread soaked in Bovril and hot water. No fancy tinned cat and dog food in those days. The animals ate what we ate, with the addition of dog biscuits for the dogs.

Bute, a black neutered male cat, came to us from 'Ferney Grotto,' the house next door whose occupants went to live in a flat in Kendal; and another cat, Tigs, was a stray who came very timidly and fed on scraps thrown out into the garden as he was too afraid at first to enter the house. He was Zelia's cat, and when she walked up to Hayfell bridge to catch the bus to work he went as far as Cross Lane with her and then returned home. By some magical means he knew when she would return in the late afternoon and he sat at the end of Cross Lane waiting for her to come down the hill.

Clever cats, all of them in their own way, and all lived to be almost twenty years of age.

CHAPTER TWENTY-FOUR

Later Village Life

Due perhaps to the fact that the Church was a mile-and-a-half away, and that the regular attenders at the Chapel were so few, there were no organisations for the women of the village to join. No Mothers' Union, Young Wives, Toddlers' Club, not even Women's Institute, and as a result there was virtually no socialising.

Women passed the time of day over the back garden fence or at the front door. In warm weather it was quite usual for all the cottage doors to be wide open, and women often sat on a hard kitchen chair in the doorway or even outside on the front step for a few minutes to enjoy the fresh air. As I have already indicated grown-ups did not go for walks, except for Aunties, and I suspect that they only went because I pestered them to go.

One or two old men stood at their front gates, leaning on them, ready to have a word with anyone who passed. One of these lived for a time next door to Aunties. His name was Joseph Atkinson, but he was always known as Joe Ak. Whatever the weather, hot or cold, he wore a black bowler hat, a collarless shirt and a grey cardigan. He had a droopy moustache that was big and white and he smoked a clay pipe.

Coffee mornings were unknown. I doubt if anyone in the village had ever tasted coffee; I certainly had not and never remember it being bought by my mother. We knew from magazines and books that coffee was served after dinner-parties but none of us had ever held, or been invited to a dinner-party, and I was sixteen years old when I drank coffee for the first time. It was 'Camp Coffee', and I did not like it at all. Camp Coffee was a concentrated liquid made of coffee and chicory, in a sauce-shaped bottle with a picture of a First World War soldier on the label. By the 1930s the image had become rather old-fashioned and it was withdrawn to be replaced by a Scotsman in a kilt.

The housewives of Mealbank had no money to spare for anything but life's necessities, and invitations to tea were issued and accepted by only a few families. Guests came from outside the village or on the fringe of it; there would be no point in asking your neighbour in for tea, besides there wasn't the time for sitting about gossiping over the tea cups. The routine household tasks, with no labour-saving devices, took up all the day for a woman with a husband and a family. The rough housework was done in the morning when old working clothes were worn: coal scuttles or buckets were filled, floors or windows washed, carpets brushed, furniture dusted and polished, bread and cakes baked and the main meal cooked. All members of the family who worked and went to school in the village came home for dinner. There was no works canteen and there were no school dinners.

After this hot midday meal had been eaten, and workers and children had returned to the Mill and to school, those who remained at home sat and waited to check their clocks by the one o'clock gun. This was an old gun which was fired from the Serpentine Woods in Kendal every day at one o'clock and could be heard quite clearly for several miles around. Its main purpose was to tell the time to people working out of doors who did not carry a watch, and to those households who had no wireless set. Having set the clocks and watches right it was the custom for women to get washed and changed into better garments. What work remained could be tackled without fear of person or clothes getting dirty. There might be ironing or mending, sewing or knitting or a little light gardening, and then tea to make.

My father spent the winter evenings reading. He bought the *Daily Mail* each day and read most of it during his lunch-hour break, and part of Sunday was taken up relaxing with the *Sunday Express*, but in the evenings he settled down with his favourite authors, Rafael Sabatini and novels of the Wild West, 'or books on farming and the countryside by A.G. Street. He could occasionally be persuaded to play a game such as snakes and ladders but not very often. It was generally accepted that after a hard day's work he must be allowed to rest and must not be disturbed. In the summer he pottered around the garden, smoking his pipe and enjoying the peace and quiet after the noise and clatter of the machines at the Mill. Both my parents were keen gardeners and on summer evenings my mother joined him in the garden. In bad weather and in the Winter she spent her evenings hand-sewing, knitting, talking to us and generally encouraging us in whatever we were doing.

The men of the village did not get together any more than the women did. There was no Public House and no other reason for meeting though several men had very small patches of garden – in the field opposite the School – where they grew vegetables.

However the outbreak of the Second World War stirred things up slightly. My father and two other men from the village were appointed Air Raid Wardens and it was necessary for them to have a Wardens' Post or meeting place. It just so happened that there was an empty house in the middle of the village and this was commandeered for the purpose. The Wardens met on several evenings a week, wearing their silver ARP badges in their lapels, and it wasn't long before a dart-board and darts found their way to the Post along with three rickety chairs, a card table and the basics in crockery and cutlery. On three evenings a week I was despatched at about 8 o'clock with a large basin of piping hot peas in a vinegary sauce, and thick chunks of bread in a basket, to keep up the Wardens' spirits as they played darts and listened for an Air Raid warning which seldom came. On the rare occasions when we did hear the Kendal siren wailing the Wardens patrolled the village and saw that everyone had their gas masks ready. On the memorable night that Barrow-in-Furness was bombed, my father and I walked onto Paddy Lane from where we could see the sky lit up from the fires started by incendiary bombs, and hear the blast like distant thunder. One black night in 1941 a single landmine was dropped a few miles north of the village. It fell onto a large and isolated farm called Cooper House and completely demolished the house and its thirteen occupants.

Television had not entered our lives, – in fact radio, or wireless as it was called then, was not a part of some people's lives at all. One or two families had a wireless set, our family being one of them. It worked from a battery – or accumulator as my father called it – and every so often this piece of equipment had to be taken to the Mill to be charged. He listened every night to the News and to talks on current affairs. The only programme we eagerly awaited was at 5.15pm each weekday, and for three-quarters-of-an-hour we sat, usually at the tea table, enthralled by Henry Hall's Dance Band. We knew by heart every note and every word of the day's popular songs, and held our breath, longing to hear our favourites, "The Man on the Flying Trapeze", "Why did she fall for the Leader of the Band?" (this one had us in ecstasy), "Who's afraid of the Big Bad Wolf?" – George Elrick singing, "The Music goes Round and Around", and Les Allen – whose photograph we had seen and with whom we were madly in love – singing "Unless", or "Alone."

My sister was six years my senior and our leisure interests had little in common. She had homework to do long before I reached that stage and when this was completed she would perhaps help with a difficult jig-saw puzzle. One interest which we shared, of fairly short duration, was make-up. I was not allowed to wear make-up until I was fourteen and then only on very special occasions. For quite a small sum of money we sent away for a make-up selection box from Max Factor, – all our favourite film stars used Max Factor face powder and lipstick. We also acquired an outfit of stage make-up, and spent hours trying it out on each other with some quite startling results.

Zelia was a keen sportswoman and in the winter joined a badminton club across at Skelsmergh, there being nothing of that sort in the village. However the one concession to social get-togethers in Mealbank was a Whist Drive which was held in the school room at regular intervals during the winter months. My parents were not interested in card games and Aunties did not really approve of them if the truth was known, but Zelia had a flair for them and hardly a Whist Drive passed without her bringing home a prize, even if it was only the Booby.

She was a very popular girl and was invited out to Dinner Dances and Hunt Balls, which I suppose were quite grand affairs for our part of the world. My mother always seemed to be making new evening gowns for these occasions and I loved to sit and watch my sister getting dressed up. I particularly remember a full-skirted long dress of pale green taffeta with big puff sleeves and a heart-shaped neckline, and another of green and silver lame with a plunging V-neck and a very tightly fitting skirt like a fish's tail.

In the Summer there was a tennis club run by the organ-playing Auntie Bessie. This operated on the fringe of the village, the first tennis court being at Logwood Mill. Then the club moved to a piece of ground between Laverock Bridge and Spital Farm where a court was made, wire netting put around and a small wooden clubhouse built. This club was far too tame for Zelia who joined a much more renowned organisation in Kendal. I played at the Mealbank club, but girls and boys of my age group could only use the court when the adults did not want it. Even for a one-eyed village club it was remarkably formal. White was almost always worn. Men and boys always wore long white trousers, and even if the ladies were not completely attired in white the only concession was perhaps a light-grey skirt worn with a white blouse and ankle socks, and of course white tennis shoes.

Skelsmergh was a very scattered parish and almost all the parishioners belonged to the farming community, but they were nevertheless more adventurous in their social activities. In addition to the badminton club they had a gathering of Church Wives, and once a fortnight a dance was held in the Church Hall. Getting to Skelsmergh, as I have said, necessitated a walk or a cycle ride of one-and-a-half miles. In windy, cold, or more especially wet weather, great was the problem of how to keep our dresses smart and our hairdo's intact on the journey to the Church Hall. Fortunately an unflattering piece of head-gear called the pixie hood had become fashionable so we were able to tuck our elaborate curls inside one of these creations, and with our dancing shoes inside our saddle bags, off we cycled.

At these Skelsmargh dances there was usually a three-piece band, – piano, violin or saxophone, and drums with a mixed bag of percussion instruments. The dances ranged from foxtrots and waltzes and the latest tango and rumba, to the old timers. *The Lancers* was a great favourite, but here one had to be very careful not to be swept completely off one's feet and whirled round at a dizzy pace with legs in the air. Supper was tea and sandwiches and a vast amount of fun and enjoyment was had without a single drop of alcohol being consumed.

We were not attracted to social activities or clubs in Kendal and so we missed, for example, joining the Girl Guides; but in any case getting to and from Kendal was a problem even after I had started cycling to school, and furthermore my parents would not allow me to cycle home alone from the town in the dark until after I had started work. So we were restricted to what games and pastimes we could think up within the village and its environs. This was not difficult, and twenty-four hours a day were never enough for all the things we wanted to do.

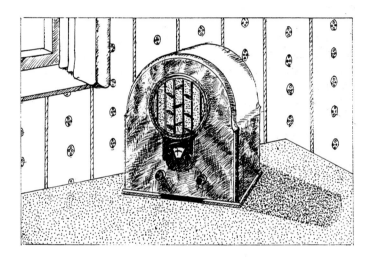

CHAPTER TWENTY-FIVE

Dialect

It was very obvious from the way we spoke that we came from the North of England, though no one but an expert could have said from precisely where.

My father was born on the border of Westmorland and Yorkshire and had lived in Westmorland all his life, and though he used many dialect words his accent was not broad. It was a similar situation with my mother. Born and brought up in a village of the West Riding of Yorkshire near the Pennines she had not the broad accent of that district as her parents had. But both my parents could be persuaded to speak in their own native dialect using words peculiar to their own particular area, and it was interesting to compare different words which had the same meaning. For example the word "sitha" in my mother's area of Yorkshire meant 'look', or 'take notice', and in Westmorland dialect it would be "looksta".

On the whole the village people and farmers round about us spoke in very broad dialect, and words like "owt" (anything), "nowt" (nothing) and "summat" (something) were in constant and general use along with "aye" (yes), "nay" (no), "nobbut" (only) and "allus" (always).

Discussing the weather, two farmers meeting might say, "turble weather", which did not mean as one might expect, 'terrible weather', – it could mean 'not bad', or even 'grand weather'. Grand was often used to describe one's state of health. "How are you feeling?" – "Grand!" – meaning 'very well'. But moderate meant just the opposite. "How is Henry?" – "Oh, only moderate", which meant 'not very well at all'.

To be fed-up or bored was to be "stalled", and "she's allus scratting and siding up" meant 'she's always fussing over domestic details and tidying up'. And a "scrow" was 'an untidy mess'. Auntie Fanny was a compulsive tidier-up and as a result of this anything left lying around for more than a few minutes was more than likely to be 'sided'. Uncle Tom had put down something he wanted to pick up again about half an hour later. It was nowhere to be seen. He searched the room for it. Eventually realisation swept over him and he exclaimed, "sided, bi God!"

Many dialect words had Danish and Viking origins, for example "laiking" was 'playing' – "Are you coming out to laik?" was a common question. "Wick" was 'lively' and "limb" was 'a lively child'. "He's a proper Limb" meant 'he's a really mischievous child". "Twining" on the other hand was 'whining' or 'complaining', and "gurning" was being cross or bad tempered. "Kysty" (ky as in 'eye') was 'too particular'. If our cat would not eat what was put in front of it my father called it "a kysty faggot".

"Fratching" meant 'quarrelling' – "They're allus fratching". "Wisht" could mean 'Be quiet!' or 'Listen!' – and "think on" meant 'Remember!' "Ligging down" meant 'lying down', and "starved" did not mean hungry or short of food but 'cold'. To say "I'm starved" meant 'I'm frozen'. "Sik" meant 'such', and "stew" meant 'upset' or 'turmoil' as in "I've nivver seen sik a stew". "Ower t'edge" was 'over the hedge', and to "frame" meant 'to tackle something properly'. If you were not doing the job right your boss might say, "Come on, frame!"

My grandparents brought their own dialect words. To be "flaid" was to be scared and "I'll warm thee" meant 'I'll scold you'. "Threng" or "throng" was 'busy', as in "she's fair throng". Mammam used to tell the peculiar tale of Throp's wife who when she wanted to commit suicide was "that throng that she had no time to look for a rope, so she hung hersel' wi' a dish clout", from which tale the saying "as thrang as Throp's wife" came into use. Another of Mammam's sayings was "as queer as Dick's hat-band", which in its entirety continued thus: Dick complained that the hat-band "went three times round and then it wouldn't tie".

Other words and sayings included "don't moider" which was 'don't worry me' or 'don't bother me', and "mardy" which meant 'petted'. "You mardy" meant 'you petted child'. If Grandpa had a cough he didn't say, 'I've got a cough': he said, "I've got a peff" – peffing was 'coughing'.

DIALECT

Losing could mean 'leaving time' as in "school is losing" – 'it is school leaving time'. Porridge was used in the plural, and referred to by Mammam as "they" or "them". When the porridge was cooked and ready to eat she would say, "they're ready".

Two small items of dialect from my father were:

> "Sticks, stayans and bayans
> And ahld yak reeats."
> (Sticks, stones and bones
> And old oak roots).

And a puzzle in the form of an addition sum:

> "Tuppence, twapence
> A groat, three 'apence
> One penny, one penny
> And an odd bawbee."

The answer to which is One Shilling.

There were local dialect names for certain members of the animal kingdom. A wren was always known as a 'chitty wren', wood lice were known as 'thrush pigs', and crane flies or Daddy-Long-Legs were 'Jinny Spinners'.

Aunties captured my imagination with the dialect poems they knew and recited, but even they could not remember all the words and therefore only fragments were passed on to me:

> "Gerraway yer crarking craters,
> Yer nivver did any good
> Yer strayed away all summer lang
> And laid i' Rowley Wood.
> And many a corn I've fetched yer up
> Wi' many a weary leg
> And when Ah cem to search yer nests
> Ah couldn't find an egg."

THE GREEN LANES

The unfinished mysterious ending of the following one had me tingling with apprehension:

> 'Yan winter's neet, Ah mind reet well,
> Our lads 'ad gone to t' fell,
> And they being tired went seean to bed,
> And Ah sat by mi sell.
> I 'eard a jike at t' winder pane
> An' deftly went to see,
> An' asking wha was jiking there,
> Says chap, "It's nobbut me!"
> "Who's me?" says I, "What wants yer here?
> Our folks is a' i' bed."
> "It's not your folks Ah want at all,
> It's thee Ah want!" he said.'

The origins of many strange sayings have been lost in the mists of time, and with the rapid growth of standard communication over the last fifty years much of our dialect has disappeared. Regional accents there are still of course, but the old dialect words must now seem like a foreign language to anyone under forty years of age.

CHAPTER TWENTY-SIX

Early Schooldays

If and when we complained about anything to do with school, my mother quickly reminded us that in her opinion if our education had been in the hands of our father we would have left school at fourteen and been sent to work at the Mill. And furthermore, she pointed out, it was the money which our Grandpa Helliwell had settled on her at her marriage which was paying for our education. This last statement was certainly a fact, but if we had attended the village school and sat the scholarship examination at the age of ten or eleven in the normal way, we would probably have passed and been able to go to the High School without having to pay the fees. The fees at the time I attended the School were four guineas a term.

The only way we could get to and from Kendal for the school day starting and finishing, short of walking there, was to catch a bus at the Shap Road end of Skelsmergh Lane. This meant walking the one-and-a-half miles each way from home. For the first week or two, when I started school, my mother took us to the lane end and saw us onto the bus. After this Zelia was held responsible for getting us there. We found the long walk tedious but never thought how much more tedious it must have been for our mother, walking twice the distance.

There was a certain amount of urgency on this early morning journey so as not to miss the bus, and with our mother to hurry us along we always reached the lane-end in plenty of time; but when we were on our own we may have sometimes dawdled on the way. From the top of the hill where stood the Church we could see the bus, half a mile away, winding its way down the Shap Road towards the lane end.

A long flight of stone steps ran down from the Church through the burial ground to the main road, and was in fact a short cut. If we were in danger of missing the bus by walking to the lane end – having seen it approaching from the hill top – down the steps we pelted and caught the bus at the bottom.

There would already be six or seven High School girls on board coming in from outlying farms, some having been brought to the bus stops by their fathers in a horse and trap.

One dreadful morning as we flew down the steps Zelia fell heavily, just as the bus reached us and we were bundled onto it. I do not remember much of what happened next except being very frightened at the sight of so much blood pouring from my sister's knee. The school staff took one look at it and immediately sent us home in a taxi. I watched from the bedroom door as Nurse, who was living with us at that time, poured iodine into the wound and swathed the knee in bandages. The wound healed eventually of course, but left a round shiny scar.

I knew all about the High School in Kendal long before I went there. Zelia had already been a pupil for some years so I was well prepared for the day in September 1932 when she took me with her for my first day, or rather my first half-day, the circumstances of this arrangement being as I have already explained. I was almost paralysed with a mixture of excitement and fear. I had already been told of several children, sisters of Zelia's contemporaries, who were in the Kindergarten and of a cousin – though just how near or distant a cousin I never knew and did not unfortu-nately bother to find out – a boy whose surname was also Robinson, whose strange Christian name was Gurth and who had white hair.

Zelia held my hand as she took me into the Kindergarten room, and there she left me. I stood alone just inside the door and looked fearfully around, wondering if anyone would speak to me. It was, in fact, Gurth who came up to me and said, "What's your name?" – and on being told he said, "O yes, we're cousins" – as though he was expecting me – and then he said, "My name is Gurth Eric Goland Robinson, but you can call me 'Gegger' (his initials GEGR), and I wash my hair with whitewash." This was pure delight and the beginning of a close and glorious friendship. Fears melted away and soon I was up to the armpits in the sand tray and loving every minute of it, under the guidance of quiet and kind Miss Jolin.

EARLY SCHOOLDAYS

There were three other boys in the KG; one, Philip, was pasty-faced, thickset, solid, and an incredibly slow mover for a young boy. He also wrote some figures and letters backwards and this brought howls of derision on his head from those of us who moved like quicksilver and were equally sharp in wits. Another boy was Brian, bespectacled, blushing, quietly spoken, who would never dare to do anything reprehensible. He was therefore a sissy. However his father was a local 'big shot', so Brian was made conductor of the KG Percussion Band.

Zelia took piano lessons but she was a half-hearted pupil. I on the other hand had pestered my mother for a year or more before I was allowed to take lessons from Miss Bittlestone. This lady was small and very thin and had a stoop, though she was not old.

It is very difficult to know what age constitutes old in the mind of a child of eight years. I suppose Miss Bittlestone was in her early thirties. She had black hair, worn in the school-mistress fashion of the day – parted in the middle and drawn back into a bun. Her complexion was very sallow and her teeth not very clean. She wore two-piece suits, silky in summer, woolly in winter, in colours which were completely uncomplimentary to her, – shades of olive or sage green, bilious yellows and greys. But she was quiet and – above all – kind and understanding and continually amazed at my rapid progress. She played the tunes on the piano for the Percussion Band and the drums, triangles, castanets and tambourines dutifully banged away in time to the beat of *When the King enjoys His own again* under the baton of Brian. (*When the King enjoys His own* what? I often wondered.) There was singing with Miss Bittlestone and dancing with Miss Foulkes, wearing my bronze-coloured dancing pumps, and together with reading and writing – in which I was already accomplished and streets ahead of my fellow pupils – I was at an enormous advantage and waited impatiently for the others to catch up.

In break times Gurth and I explored unfrequented and exciting corners of the school grounds around the greenhouses and potting sheds. We searched for interesting leaves and seed-heads and poked about amongst the piles of plant pots and gardening tools, sometimes finding a frog which had strayed into the gardens from the canal head which was on the other side of the high wall.

Gurth's father was what my parents called, "a gentleman farmer" – in other words he worked at a distance from the muck of the farm and wore smart tweed suits and brogue shoes instead of collarless shirts, old jackets, fustian trousers and boots caked with cow dung like the farmers around Mealbank. He also wrote a weekly farming column in the Westmorland Gazette under the pen name of *Agricola*. He and his wife, I had been told at home, were first cousins and there had been some anxiety on the part of their families at their determination to marry. When Gurth and I met up again in our teens and became rather more than just good friends, his family – who had by now moved to Skipton – seemed equally anxious that he and I should not become too closely involved with one another.

This short and blissful period during our time in the KG soon came to an end with the departure of Miss Jolin and the arrival of Miss MacKinlay. This woman was small and stocky. She had a large bottom which bounced up and down as she walked even though, or perhaps because, it was always encased in very tight skirts. Her mouth was permanently drawn down in a disapproving and sour expression. When she asked for our names, Gurth said, his blue eyes bright and twinkling, "We're brother and sister", and of course she believed him. How long it was before she discovered that we were not in fact brother and sister I never knew, because she did not refer to it, but I have often wondered if this incident set her against me and caused me untold misery for the rest of my school life. During that time of being seven and eight years old she singled me out for punishment – to stand in the corner for long periods or to be kept in at break time – my only crime being to chatter when I should have been quiet. It was almost as though she resented the abilities of one who had so mischievously taken her in.

EARLY SCHOOLDAYS

Boys left the Kindergarten, and the school, at the age of eight so I no longer had Gurth to support me, but I had moved from the KG myself by then, up to the Lower Third Form in the Main School. The sand tray, the dolls and the percussion band were left behind, and proper school work began in earnest.

CHAPTER TWENTY-SEVEN

Later Schooldays

At school we were taught to pass exams, and we did just that. I do not remember either Zelia or myself ever failing an exam. Much of what I was taught was extremely boring, the Old Testament prophets and Scott's *The Talisman* at the age of ten and eleven for example, but even though there was little of what now would be called self-expression we had an excellent grounding in subjects which, I have come to realise, mattered.

I have to confess however that neither my sister nor I found the academic side of school life particularly agreeable. Zelia's interests lay mainly on the sports field though she enjoyed Art and also Geography, where there were plenty of maps to draw. Mine were in Music and English Literature (in spite of *The Talisman*) and I used what I learned at school to further my interests at home.

School was not an entirely happy place for either of us, and it is not difficult to see why. The headmistress at that time was a snob; an uncompromising vegetarian, an animal-loving fanatic, and a sadist – but for all that she was also a very creditable teacher, though this was hardly a suitable cocktail of virtues and vices for the Head of a girls' school. Pre-eminent with her were girls whose fathers were clergymen, doctors, lawyers or in big business. These girls, through no fault of their own let it be said, were her favourites. This favouritism was not shown by other members of staff though some were clearly influenced by it. Girls like ourselves who were the daughters of tradesmen, small shop-keepers or farmers, came low in the pecking order.

This snobbery permeated insidiously through all school activities. We were aware of it, felt it, and found it difficult to understand and to accept, particularly as we were fee-payers and our parents could afford to buy, in addition to our large wardrobe of uniform and sports clothes, all the extra equipment we needed for specialist subjects such as

Art, Biology, Music and various sports, – and of course all our books, none of which were provided by the school. Perhaps it was this which made us both, and me in particular, rebellious and reluctant to conform to the school rules as we grew older.

The High School uniform had always been predominantly green. In the early 1930s we wore pleated green tunics tied with a red girdle; this was over a white blouse and a green tie which had KHS embroidered on it in red and white silk. We wore green winter coats, long brown stockings, and small and close-fitting pull-on green hats. In summer we wore green blazers and cream Panama hats.

Later in the 1930s the uniform underwent modernisation. The tunic lost its pleats and acquired a more fashionable line; the collar and tie disappeared and were replaced by a square-necked and cream-coloured blouse, and the pull-on hat gave way to a green beret or a velour hat with a brim. I of course had both styles of hat but favoured the velour, which was definitely a classier and more expensive piece of headgear than any other.

This uniform was obligatory for the Autumn and Spring terms. In the Summer term dresses could be worn with white ankle socks – but there was no uniform style or colour until the late 1930s when a plain green dress with a white collar, or a green-and-white striped dress were introduced. White socks were banished and we had to be bare-legged and wear brown sandals.

My mother, no doubt along with many other mothers, was outraged by the shapelessness of the frocks. "Washerwomen's dresses" she called them until one day not long after the arrival of a new Head Mistress an announcement was made to the effect that we could wear any style of dress within reason, providing it was green or green and white.

My mother moved like lightning. The very next day down she went to Musgrove's in Kendal, bought two dress patterns and two different lengths of material, and sewing far into the night produced a new dress for me to wear two days after the announcement, and a second dress two days after that. The following week, in the middle of a lesson, the school secretary entered the classroom and asked me to go to the Head's sitting room. All faces were turned towards me. What had I done wrong this time? Indeed I wondered myself what it could be.

However on entering the Head's room I was astonished to be confronted by a rather weak smile. "The dresses I had been, and was at that moment, wearing: where had my mother bought them? In Kendal? How well made they were! What good material! What a lovely style! Would I mind telling her where they had come from?" When I told her that my mother had made them she was clearly very surprised, though why she should be I found difficult to understand. It must have been, of course, that I was so accustomed to everything I wore being hand-made and she no doubt bought all her clothes ready-made. That was all. I was dismissed from The Presence with another sickly smile. The best part of the whole affair was the pride and pleasure it gave my mother to be complimented on her choice of material and patterns, and her sewing expertise.

Outings from School were rare and therefore especially welcome. The Lancaster to Kendal canal was just outside the furthest boundary of the school grounds, and Castle Mills Race – an artificial diversion of the River Kent – flowed past the front gates. As a six-year-old in the Kindergarten we were taken Nature Walks along the canal and river banks, looking at plants and wildlife and fishing for interesting items in the water with a seaside fishing net, all to be written about and illustrated with drawings on our return to the classroom.

Once a week, on a Monday afternoon, we walked in crocodile to a swimming lesson. Different school forms went on different days at different times so Zelia and I did not meet on these occasions, but I heard the tale one day over the tea-table at home – amid gales of laughter – how on the walk to the baths the elastic in her knickers had broken and they had fallen down around her ankles. Apparently she had had the presence of mind to step quickly out of them and put them in her pocket.

THE GREEN LANES

The local indoor swimming baths were housed in Allhallows Lane in the centre of the town. Originally the Public Baths and Wash-Houses, this solid mid-Victorian edifice with its tall chimney gave no immediate hint from the outside as to what lay within and below ground level.

Mrs Guinea taught us swimming, and I remember well that on my first visit to the Baths – no doubt seeing the apprehension in my face in the echoing and chlorine-smelling atmosphere – she carried me in her arms into the shallow end and dipped me, a little at a time, into the water. She reckoned confidently that she would have me swimming in a couple of weeks, but in fact it took much longer than that because I was really quite frightened of the water, though as I have said elsewhere the river and the sea held no terrors for me.

After a session in the Baths my mother met me and took me to Dodd's cafe for a good tea. In later years, when I was older and too embarrassed to be met, I was given money to buy something to eat; it was my mother's firm belief that after being immersed in water the body needed food. It being a school rule that we were not allowed to eat out of doors in public places, wearing school uniform, what I bought to eat had to wait to be consumed until I had either boarded the bus to go home or had cycled out of the town onto the open road.

It must have been just before the War that an exchange of English teachers was arranged. Miss Pride, an attractive Scots woman who I greatly admired, went to America for a year and in exchange a dinky, dainty little person called Miss Jack came to us. During her year at KHS I was asked by the Geography mistress if a visit for the class to Mealbank Mill could be arranged. Miss Jack was invited to accompany us as she had not seen the process of turning raw wool into cloth.

The only means of transport to the Mill would be by bicycle, and those who did not have a bike would have to borrow one. Some people were not very proficient riders either and for some days before the visit they could be seen practising around the school paths, Miss Jack included.

The ride from the School to the Mill was uneventful – in spite of some rather alarming wobbling on the way – until the final few yards when Miss Jack fell from her bicycle just outside the Mill Offices. Fortunately she was unhurt, though her beautiful grey suede shoes and flawless silk stockings were damaged.

On arrival we were split up into three groups. Uncle Tom took one group, my father took the second group – which of course I contrived to be part of – and a colleague of his took the third group. I was very proud of my father on this occasion. Somehow it made up a little for my own inadequacies and inability to do something useful and positive at school.

In spite of the trials of my school life, there were of course many good things to remember in those seven years from the Lower Third to the Sixth Form.

I suppose that in the 1930s the school grounds covered about three acres. I do not remember any of it being out of bounds and we were free to play or wander about anywhere, outside lesson times; however venturing outside the school grounds was strictly forbidden.

From my earliest explorations with Gurth I had loved all the corners and all aspects of what were once the private gardens of the elegant houses of Kent Terrace (later renamed Thorny Hills), some of which became the School itself. It was incidentally in one of these houses – which became Kentdale Nursing Home – that I was born. I never tired of the walks around the tennis courts nor of the massive copper beech tree, or the fir tree (which was the only one we were allowed to climb), or the Summer House on 'D' Court and the track around 'A' Court, nor of playing Hopscotch on the Hard Court.

Our mid-morning break meant buns. A tray of iced finger-buns was manned by two prefects outside the gymnasium. Buns cost a penny each and when the bell sounded, heralding break-time, we ran full tilt to be as near to the head of the queue as possible and ensure a bun to have with our daily bottle of milk. If we were among the first five or six in the queue there might even be a choice of icing, as occasionally there were half-a-dozen chocolate iced buns amongst the others.

It has always been fashionable to complain about school dinners. We moaned about a kind of hot-pot which we called Bone Stew, about Spotted Dog, about Dead Man's Leg and about Boiled Baby, and in fact some of us moved from the meat-eating tables to one of the two vegetarian tables instituted by the non-meat-eating Head at that time. We were certainly not vegetarians, but that food seemed to us more attractive and indeed some of it was: rich bean casseroles, cheese and rice cutlets, eggs Mornay, and some nutty concoctions. A prefect or a member of staff sat at the head of each table and served out the food. We dreaded the (fortunately) infrequent occasions when the French mistress took the head of the table because then it was, "parlez en Français, s'il vous plaît, toujours en Français," and conversation virtually ceased.

But in spite of our complaints the food was good and we ate most of it. Only girls who lived near to the school went home for dinner so the greater proportion of pupils had the school meal, and catering for up to two hundred girls after the War started must have been anything but easy. In fact the Second World War would bring many changes to school life.

CHAPTER TWENTY-EIGHT

End of Schooldays

The mid-1930s saw the discontinuation of the privately run bus service which carried the Mill workers to and from Kendal. The buses were of ancient vintage even then, two brown-coloured, shuddering vehicles no longer serviceable or reliable. The service was taken over and run by Ribble, the largest bus company operating in the county. This meant that anyone could now travel on what became known locally as the Mill bus. We were thus released from the long trail to and from Skelsmergh Lane end; now all we had to do was to run down the hill to the Mill yard.

The bus left the Mill at 8.15am, which meant that we were amongst the first to arrive at school, and we were often the last to leave as the bus taking us home did not depart from the stop near the railway station until 5.15pm.

But as I have related elsewhere, at the age of twelve or thirteen I began cycling to school. This coincided with the outbreak of the Second World War and with the end of Zelia's school days and her compulsory registration for War work. With this a major change took place in the pattern of my school attendance.

The first thing was that I was no longer answerable to my older sister during school hours. Our paths had rarely crossed, but I knew that I had to watch my P's and Q's (whatever they were) so that I did not let her down by anything I said, or by my behaviour, which she may find necessary to repeat to our mother. I did not now either have to wait for her on some occasions, or hurry up on others, so that we could travel home together. I was now uninhibited, which may or may not have been a good thing.

I was almost thirteen when the War started. My parents like thousands of others knew that it was coming, and on the Sunday morning that it was announced I was sent out of the house and not allowed to listen to the wireless when Mr Chamberlain spoke to the nation at eleven o'clock on the

THE GREEN LANES

Third of September 1939. I walked alone up the Big Hill, my gas-mask round my neck, feeling rather afraid. I looked up into the sky, wondering if German aeroplanes would shatter the quietness and kill us all with their bombs.

But of course it was the children in the industrial towns and cities who were most at risk from German bombs, and it was not long before a small group of them from South Shields arrived in the village, and suddenly we all became familiar with a new word, "evacuees".

A few days before they arrived my mother was appointed Billeting Officer for the area. This meant that she had to visit the houses in the village and the nearby farms to see how many spare bedrooms there were. By law any unoccupied bedrooms could be used to accommodate evacuees whether the house-holders liked it or not.

The children arrived early one evening with their teachers on a bus. They were travel-stained and tired. Many of them were very young and I remember thinking how lost and apprehensive they looked, as well they might, taken with hardly any warning from their mothers and their homes and all the familiar noise and bustle of the city, to be planted in the house of complete strangers in a small quiet village a hundred miles away.

My mother had to decide, with some help and advice from the teachers, which children would be most suitable to go to the homes available. Even Aunties found themselves in charge of a shy little six-year-old girl, and we at School House took in two sisters – then aged only four and six – who lived with us for nearly four years.

It was generally assumed throughout the country that there would be air-raids, and possibly gas attacks in those early days and weeks of the War, so gas masks had to be carried everywhere. When they were first issued they were packed in cardboard boxes and hung or carried by a piece of string. This became impractical for obvious reasons, and very soon in the shops one could buy gas mask cases in an amazing variety of shapes, designs and materials. We hung them round our necks and shoulders as we moved about, and while in lessons slung them on the backs of our chairs.

END OF SCHOOLDAYS

We had mock Air-Raid drill, and when the siren sounded each class marched quickly to a designated safe place. Ours was the stationery cupboard which was just about large enough for twenty-five to thirty girls to squeeze into. We sat cross-legged on the floor under the shelves which held reams of paper and piles of new exercise books, until the All-Clear sounded, wearing our gas mask which made rude noises when our breath was expelled through them.

The school curriculum was certainly affected and the whole atmosphere became unsettled. Some younger members of staff were called up into the Services and others volunteered. They were replaced in some cases by women who came out of retirement, but we were left without a teacher of piano and violin. This teacher was not replaced and those of us who took lessons on these instruments were left high and dry.

I scouted around for some time before finding Mr Dalrymple, the organist of the Parish Church in Kendal, to give me piano lessons. As his name suggests, he was a Welshman – fairly elderly – and gave the impression that teaching me was a trial to him. It probably was. Being taught by him was a trial as well. He made me play scales with pennies on the back of my hands, and if they fell off he rapped my knuckles with a ruler. When I complained he replied unrelentingly that I could consider myself lucky he had not made me play with wine glasses on my hands. But he taught me to play Grieg, which was a refreshing change from Handel, Beethoven and Mozart.

Literature and music were my main interests both at school and at home. I was a voracious reader and a regular borrower of books at the Public Library. During school holidays it was not unusual for me to read a book a day. I featured in most school plays, usually type-cast in the role of a princess or any female character where long golden hair was required. My interests were fuelled by visits from the Old Vic Theatre Company and the Sadlers Wells Opera Company who came to St George's Theatre in Kendal. Hundreds of school children attended matinée performances specially put on for us, and having been prepared in class beforehand for what we were going to see we were able to understand and enjoy the plays and the operas to the full, savouring the comedy in *Figaro* and *The Barber* and weeping copiously over the death of Violetta in *Traviata*.

Other memorable musical events were a piano recital by Benno Moisewitch during which a string in the grand piano broke with a loud report. The maestro carried on the performance apparently unperturbed. I also attended a song recital by Dame Maggie Teyte, the outstanding item for me being her rendering of " Oft in the Stilly Night". I remember a local eccentric gentleman, attired in a long black overcoat and flowing white silk scarf, standing up in his box applauding and calling out, 'Encore! Encore!' All these experiences were new and rather strange to us. It was the first time that we had had the opportunity of seeing professional actors, singers and musicians live on the stage. These were occasions which made a profound impression on me and which I have never forgotten.

Another war-time activity in school, in complete contrast to anything cultural, was a type of allotment gardening. Among the many posters exhorting the public to do this or not to do that was the one which urged us to Dig for Victory. So a piece of waste ground at the base of Castle Hill, bordering on the hockey pitch, was turned into allotments and two girls shared each plot. Some of the fathers, including mine, were roped in for help and advice and came down on Saturday afternoons to give their expert suggestions and opinions. We actually produced some reasonable (if very ordinary) vegetables.

But the future was uncertain. Going to college or to university somehow did not seem as important or as attractive as it had done a year or two ago. So what was I to do after leaving school? I had already gained a Distinction and five Credits in School Certificate at the age of fourteen. Entering the Sixth Form one could choose the subjects to study for Higher School Certificate; I chose English, Art, French and Biology – a curious mixture. As our Biology mistress remarked, "well, Betty, you could write a Biology book, do your own illustrations and translate it into French".

END OF SCHOOLDAYS

Being in the Sixth Form provided a few perks. We no longer sat at a desk in a class room but in pairs in cubicles down one of the corridors looking into the quadrangle. French lessons with Miss Jenkins were held in the Staff sitting-room, in big armchairs in front of a roaring coal fire in Winter, and outside under the copper beech in Summer. And we were allowed out into the town during the lunch break.

But I was restless, not knowing what I wanted to do. Zelia had been Called Up and had gone away to train as an inspector of aircraft parts in Manchester, and it was after I had had a year and part of a term in the Sixth Form that the librarian of the local Public Library wrote to the Head to ask if there was a girl who might be interested in a career in Librarianship, and that a post in the Library was vacant. I was given a letter to take to my mother suggesting that I might be suitable for the post, and that the school would be willing to release me at once. Not only willing, I thought, but glad to release me.

My mother took some persuading, but it just so happened that her private nest egg of money had almost run out and the prospect of not having to pay school fees and all the extras, and of a little cash coming in from what I could earn, was very attractive. She must also have realised that I was serving no useful purpose by staying on at school, and what was she going to do with me when eventually I had to leave?

So it was decided. The Library wanted me to start at once. My exit from school life was unremarkable and unnoticed. I cycled away from school one afternoon in the middle of the Autumn Term and never returned.

No tears. They would come later. But disappointment that no-one, neither staff nor girls, had said "Goodbye", or "Good Luck". Defiance, always near the surface, made me toss my head and say that I did not care and that it was marvellous to have got away.

And I was relieved to have left behind me a situation which mainly due to the War was clearly going nowhere. I was starting work, beginning a new chapter, meeting fresh people.

THE GREEN LANES

School life was over. But more significantly than that, childhood was over. The wonder and excitement of the countryside and the changing seasons would never be quite the same again. I would see it all differently. Never again would I have the time to stand and absorb it. Other friends and other pursuits would claim me and the childhood I was leaving behind would gradually be consigned to memory there to lie dormant waiting to be re-awakened.

Epilogue

Memories rise and fall imperceptibly, like the treacherous tides we knew on the estuary. The water creeps in soundlessly, lapping at the shoreline until the tide is full and high in a silvery light.

So images gather into the consciousness when the first warmth of Spring is felt, and with the first signs of new growth, transporting the mind and spirit to the lanes and woods to search again for the nest of a thrush or blackbird; to pick the first bluebells and to run home with them already wilting in hot little hands; to know again the heady, intoxicating smell of Summer from the grass verges, the fields and the hedges full of blossom; to lie in the long warm-scented grass making daisy chains, and to follow the haycart piled high as it sways along the lane to the farm.

There is an aching and a longing for the colours and the falling leaves of Autumn; to wander along the wood paths when the birds have fallen silent and the hazel nuts are ripe for picking, when the wind tears the leaves from the trees and they fall to add another layer to the woodland floor, knowing that the slowly rotting layers will be added to year after year, layer upon layer unceasingly when I can no longer return; and for the silence of the clear star-laden skies of Winter, the smoke from the cottage chimneys, and the welcome of the warm fireside and hot toast for tea.

The images recede like the ebbing of the tide, and as they fade I am left with an empty sadness, recalling the carefree days and the now shadowy faces which have gone for ever. But I am thankful to have experienced as a child the tranquillity of the unspoilt countryside, to have been aware of the wonder and the richness of the natural world all around me, and to have known the love of those nearest to me.

The burial-ground now bears witness to them all. Those whose lives were long, and those who were tragically cut down in their best years. They lie in this quiet, wind-blown place, their headstones grey and lichen-covered, surrounded by fields and by the distant hills.

THE GREEN LANES

I can return now without heartache. I can walk the green lanes and look across the woods up to Benson Knott, or across the fields to the river and the bridge. I can pass through the graveyard dry-eyed, and as I turn towards home I know that what I experienced was a childhood idyll. This will remain my enduring memory; untouched by changes wrought over the years, unmoved by strangers I now meet in the old familiar places, undaunted by the relentless passing of time and uplifted by all that I have inherited.

APPENDIX

Mealbank Mills

Of the four different mills which have been recorded, three were in a group in the village and the fourth a short distance downstream, and originally referred to as Scarfoot Mill but known to us as Logwood Mill.

Exploring as a child along the river between the village and Logwood, when the water was low, brought to my attention the remnants of a stone building which my father assured me were the remains of a bobbin mill. This was quite feasible as there were any number of bobbin mills in Westmorland; but it may have been the ruin of an older mill, said by Robert Long of Scarfoot (who worked at Logwood and was a contemporary of my grandparents) to have been started in 1713 to grind dyewoods for the textile trade which, as its name implies, was the purpose of Logwood Mill itself.

The group of three mills in the village were:

a) The Woollen Mill. The earliest records of this mill go back to 1767, the owners between then and 1838 being Broadbent and then Gibson. In 1838 George and Isaac Braithwaite, who owned both a drysalting business in Kendal and Logwood Mill, took it over. The mill was rebuilt on a slightly different site and was powered by a large water wheel which was replaced by a turbine in 1895. In 1920 the mill race was altered and a larger turbine installed. Because of this the weir for the next mill downstream (Logwood) was removed, and that mill closed.

b) The Corn Mill. This was on the site of the woollen mill office building and was in operation during the nineteenth century. The road between the offices and the village was known as Corn Mill Lane.

c) The Snuff Mill. A small corner of the woollen mill building was leased to Samuel Gawith and Co. as a snuff mill from 1792 to 1921. Until about 1950 this firm's name was visible on the door of the building at Snuff Mill Corner.

I have been told that somewhere near the snuff mill there was once an oil mill, presumably for grinding linseed, but I have no proof of this.

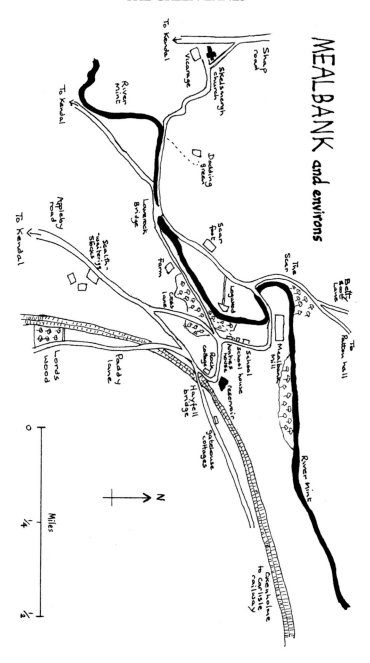

MEALBANK and environs